IMAGES
of America

CAPE FEAR
LOST

It might look like a park, but this is South Third Street, looking north near the intersection at Dock, c. 1880. The chimney and fence of the Edward Kidder House can be seen on the right. A portion of the MacRae-Dix House is visible on the left. (1776.55.55.)

Cover: The anachronistic cover shot, photographed by Louis T. Moore at the 1928 Feast of Pirates parade, showcases Wilmington's Third Street and sets the tone for looking back.

IMAGES
of America

CAPE FEAR LOST

Susan Taylor Block

ARCADIA
PUBLISHING

Copyright © 1999 by Cape Fear Museum Associates
ISBN 9781531601225

Published by Arcadia Publishing
Charleston, South Carolina

Library of Congress Catalog Card Number: 2004117211

FFor all general information contact Arcadia Publishing at:
Telephone 843-853-2070
Fax 843-853-0044
E-mail sales@arcadiapublishing.com
For customer service and orders:
Toll-Free 1-888-313-2665

Visit us on the Internet at www.arcadiapublishing.com

*This book is dedicated to Hugh Morton:
native to Wilmington, claimed by the state.*

This Market Street scene looks east from Seventh, c. 1903. During the 18th century, a public hanging ground existed on this block, but later, elegant houses graced the north side of Market Street, between Seventh and Eighth. (1980.21.6.)

Contents

Acknowledgments		6
Introduction		7
1.	Home Sweet Homes	9
2.	Cape Fear Foundations	49
3.	The Marketplace	79
4.	Along the Shore	113
Bibliography		125
Photograph Donors		126
Index		126

ACKNOWLEDGMENTS

A number of individuals contributed to this publication. Janet K. Seapker, who conceived the idea, also was a valuable source of information. Others who contributed professional services, facts, or memories are Timothy Bottoms, Dana Twersky, G. Case Newberry, Barbara Rowe, Grace Russ, Harry Warren, Edward F. Turberg, Beverly Tetterton, Joe Sheppard, Hugh MacRae II, Dr. Chris Fonvielle, Barbara Marcroft, Bill Reaves, Tony P. Wrenn, Diane Cashman, Dr. James Rush Beeler, Nancy Beeler, Merle Chamberlain, Allan T. Strange, Jonathan Noffke, Jerry Cotten, Dr. Wilson Angley, Steve Massengill, Anne Russell, Isabel James Lehto, Peter Browne Ruffin, Walter Hunt, Tom Grainger, Col. Edward P. Bailey, Gibbs Willard, Martin Willard, Neal Thomas, Joe Bennett, the late Maxine Dizor, Linda Upperman Smith, Bart Smyth, Jean McKoy Graham, William Childs, James Price, Myrtle May Padrick, Henry B. Rehder, James Moss Burns Jr., John H. Debnam, Walker Taylor III, Mary Wootten, Brooks N. Preik, James A. Locke Miller Jr., Lillian B. Boney, Leslie N. Boney Jr., Tabitha Hutaff McEachern, Virginia Jennewein, John Murchison, Dorothy T. Page, Tony Rivenbark, Anna Pennington, Edwin Borden, Sigmond Bear, William Sutton, Frances S. Lee, Judy Perdew French, Joseph W. Taylor Jr., Betty Hill Taylor, Bill Creasy, Catherine Solomon, Sandra Corbett Hiatt, Joanne Corbett, Rebecca Laymon, Mary Harriss, Betty B. Crouch, Robert Neale, Henry Longley, Catherine Rhett Fox, Cathy Myerow, David E. Block, William Bentley Block, Mona Smalley, Sue Boney Ives, Martha McAllister, Fred Sternberger, Sadie Hood, Jay Hammer, Rosalie Carr, and the late Emma Woodward MacMillan, who earlier wrote a book, *Wilmington's Vanished Homes and Buildings*. The archives of the Lower Cape Fear Historical Society and the local history materials at the New Hanover County Public Library have yielded many facts. William M. Reaves's newspaper clipping files deserve special praise.

I would like especially to thank Suzanne Nash Ruffin, who edited *Cape Fear Lost* with her usual diamond-tipped pen; Ann Hewlett Hutteman for reviewing the manuscript; Cape Fear Museum photographer extraordinaire Melva Pearsall Calder; and my husband, Frederick L. Block, for sharing his knowledge and for being such good and entertaining company on countless field trips.

INTRODUCTION

For there are deeds that should not pass away, and names that must not wither.
—Plaque in St. Philip's Church, Brunswick Town

Though New Hanover County has lost distinctive and important buildings to fire, wind, and water, it is those lost in the name of "progress" that most sadden preservationists. In 1939, when citizens of Wilmington considered tearing down the city hall itself, reserved historian Elizabeth F. McKoy responded in a most uncharacteristic way. She wrote an article for the local newspaper using images of dreams in which her grandfather, uncle, and father spoke to her about the value of historic preservation.

"Child," said her long-dead grandfather, Henry Bacon, a U.S. government engineer, "Why are you letting them tear down that town hall? There is an interesting fire prevention used in that building. On the second floor, between the double flooring, there is a layer of sand through which fire cannot eat."

Then the ghostly voice of her uncle, Henry Bacon Jr., spoke to her. Though he had left Wilmington to pursue a career in architecture that would include designing the Lincoln Memorial, he studied the city hall every time he visited. "The columns are unsurpassed in their true Corinthian proportions. It will not be destroyed without danger to Wilmington's sense of values and a loss which her sons and daughters will never forgive," he said.

Then her father, William Beery McKoy, implored, probably much as he had in life, "Wilmington has always been a town that has torn down its old buildings. The people were not of one mind among themselves as were those of Charleston. In the 1890s, our old town cut down the trees that lined Front Street—and why? Because New York did not have trees on its business streets! We had iron balconies on old brick buildings, iron fences and iron gates and ventilators of intricate and lovely design. No one saved them. No one realized their beauty. Now this town hall!"

Suddenly, Elizabeth McKoy's dreamlike state was interrupted when her flesh-and-blood brother walked through the door, speaking words full of forebodin, "I wish Wilmingtonians knew what the makers of pictures thought of this building they are talking about tearing down," said James H. McKoy. "I was just with the vice-president of International Motion Pictures Corporation. We'd just driven into Wilmington and he almost shouted, 'Look at that building!' He stopped his car, got out, and without another word, took pictures of it. Not content with a few, he took a whole roll of film. That man had traveled from coast to coast—yet here in our little tucked away town, he'd found a sight to enthuse him."

Indeed, now that Wilmington has become a location for the international production of motion pictures, the whole world views our scenic city. But for viewers, visitors, and especially residents, there could have been so much more to see, to study, and to cherish. Though the city hall survived, "progress" thrived for decades before ardent preservationists, echoing thoughts similar to Elizabeth McKoy's, could prevail.

Cape Fear Lost showcases a special part of Cape Fear Museum's photograph collection, while also sharing photographs housed at the Lower Cape Fear Historical Society, the New Hanover County Public Library, the library of the University of North Carolina, Duke University Library, North Carolina Division of Archives and History, and private collections. Cape Fear Museum invites the reader to embark on a bittersweet photographic voyage.

North Front Street looks south in this 1908 photograph. Signs at Princess Street reading, "View the Ocean," or "Lumina," beckon passengers to board the beachcar for the star attraction at Wrightsville Beach. Past the Orton Hotel (right foreground), the towers of the four-story Masonic Hall and the 1879 City Market punctuate the western sky. (North Carolina Division of Archives and History.)

One

Home Sweet Homes

"A person would naturally consider that Wilmington being so near the sea coast, and located in the sandy region, would be level and flat. But this is not so. Every street is beautifully undulating and nearly all of them are well shaded. The suburban residences and those out of the heart of the city are built in a pretty style of architecture and are surrounded with tasteful, well-kept grounds. A stroll out of town from any street will repay the sightseer," stated the *Wilmington Messenger*, July 14, 1887. Of course, in 1887, almost everything in today's Wilmington would have been considered "out of town." Even within the narrow confines of our commercial downtown area, handsome residences once abounded. What has survived is dominated by Italianate-style architecture, but what is gone is diverse, distinct, and often delightful.

In 1910, with no Internet chat rooms or television, the front porch was a social gathering place. Members of the Robert H. Bowden family are pictured here at their home at 415 Princess Street. This location is now dominated by a BellSouth office building. (1992.103.16.)

Russellborough, located on the northern border of Brunswick Town, was described by historian Lawrence Lee as "the most historic of all early Cape Fear dwellings." Roger Moore sold the Russellborough property, once part of Orton, to Captain John Russell in 1751. Russell, captain of H.M. Sloop's *Scorpion*, began building a house but died before it was completed. The Moore family regained the property after Captain Russell's wife died.

In 1753, Arthur Dobbs of Carrickfergus, Northern Ireland, was appointed royal governor of North Carolina. He moved first to New Bern, but never was happy there. On March 1, 1758, he purchased the 55-acre Russellborough tract for five shillings and one peppercorn. Though the house was just a "shell," the 68-year-old governor moved in immediately and began "planting, and building, draining, and fencing."

He soon named the place "Castle Dobbs," after his home in Carrickfergus, Northern Ireland. However, unlike the solid stone structure he once lived in, this house was built " . . . after the West Indian manner with double galleries or piazzas." Dobbs added a fine stable, a coach house, and various other outbuildings, leading Governor Tryon to note Russellborough as the "house which has so many assistances."

A dedicated amateur botanist, Governor Dobbs was amazed and delighted to find the Venus' flytrap growing at Castle Dobbs. He arranged the shipment of specimens to naturalists in the British Isles. "I have taken a little Plantation at the sound on the sea coast," wrote Governor Dobbs. "We have a kind of Catch Fly Sensitive which closes upon any thing that touches it. It grows in Latitude 34 but not in 35."

Arthur Dobbs died in 1765 and William Tryon succeeded him. He rented the Dobbs home for a period of time and finally, on February 12, 1767, Arthur Dobbs's son, Captain Edward Brice

Dobbs, sold the 55-acre tract to Governor William Tryon for 300 pounds. The new governor quickly changed the name to Bellfont. But Tryon was as unhappy in Brunswick as Dobbs had been in New Bern. Even before purchasing Bellfont, he had worked with English architect John Hawks to plan an elegant official residence, which would be known as Tryon Palace.

After Governor Tryon moved to New Bern in 1770, he sold Bellfont to William Dry, a wealthy planter and collector of the port. The elegant house was burned by the British in the spring of 1776. This depiction of Bellfont, based on descriptions in the *Colonial Records*, is part of a mural painted by local artist Ronald Williams for Wilmington resident Bob Jenkins.

Cornelius Harnett, a member of the Continental Congress, built Maynard c. 1752 on a picturesque bluff near the spot where Smith Creek empties into the Cape Fear River. An avenue of hardy live oaks lined the drive to the 12-room house; its interior was paneled in red cedar. On May 31, 1784, widow of Cornelius, Mary Harnett sold Maynard to John Hill, who renamed it Hilton. From that point on, Hilton was home to a sequence of Hills and Wrights, who were longtime relatives. Hilton was destroyed c. 1900. (1968.17.2.)

Attorney John Burgwin, best known today as builder of the Burgwin-Wright House, was born in Wales and moved to Wilmington by way of Charleston. He owned five ships and several local businesses; in addition, he served as Governor Arthur Dobbs's personal secretary. In 1753, he married a local girl, Margaret Haynes, granddaughter of the Reverend Richard Marsden, who had purchased 640 acres of land from Maurice Moore. Marsden's son-in-law Roger Haynes lived in a house said to have resembled a miniature castle. The house became known as Castle Haynes, an area name that still exists, albeit in altered form. When John Burgwin obtained Castle Haynes, he hired an English architect to enlarge and embellish the old Marsden House. When the work was completed, Burgwin's country home was a 17-room house that measured 150 feet wide and 30 feet deep. It had two large wings, each sided with choice cypress shingles made by Col. Samuel Ashe. The house was heated by nine fireplaces and fitted with elaborate finishing work. A detached brick library, sizable enough to contain a "large number of books, chairs and tables," was used also as a family chapel. The property, which had long planted corn, rice, indigo, and cotton, expanded to 2,000 acres and sported 10 acres of "garden and pleasure grounds." The stables housed 20 horses.

After the death of his first wife, John Burgwin began to call the house "The Hermitage," an ironic name. The "Travelers' Room," a shed that had been finished and appended to the south wing, could have used a revolving door. In addition to having a stockpile of Madeira, "the urbanity of Mr. Burgwin's manner, the liberality of his habits, his general information, and cheerful disposition could not fail of attracting both daily and often weekly guests." Many of the host's married male friends used the house as a weekend retreat, especially for merchants who often spent Sundays there.

While engaged in a game of blind man's buff on January 8, 1775, in the Long Hall of the Hermitage, John Burgwin fell and broke a leg. Orthopedic travail afforded him a hobbling exit from economic and political uncertainties inherent in the last months of the American Revolution. A local surgeon prescribed a change of climate, and Burgwin sailed to Bristol,

England, five months after his accident. Before departing, he asked Elizabeth deRosset, widow of Armand, to watch over The Hermitage from the deRosset country estate next door, possibly the old Haynes Castle. Vigilance could not keep British soldiers from plundering Burgwin's mansion or the new government from confiscating all his local real estate. John Burgwin returned to North Carolina with his new bride, Eliza Bush Burgwin; though 21 years his junior, she had been born the same day and hour as her husband. His plantation was restored to him in 1779, but not his fortune. He drowned at The Hermitage in the shallow waters of Prince George Creek in May 1803.

Burgwin family members continued to live at The Hermitage for the next 100 years, but found it necessary eventually to subdivide a portion of the property. In 1872, 3,000 acres of land were set aside and sold in 5-acre tracts. About the same time, several bodies from The Hermitage cemetery were disinterred and buried at Oakdale, including that of Captain J.H.K. Burgwin and John Burgwin's grandson, who had died heroically in the Mexican War. Moving Captain Burgwin's gravemarker was an ordeal noted in the local newspaper, "The splendid monument erected at Castle Hayne over the body of J.H.K. Burgwin, of the first regiment, U.S. Dragoons, has been removed to this city by Mr. G.W.W. Davis and others and was placed in Oakdale where the body had been previously interred. This monument is said to be one of the largest in the cemetery."

On March 31, 1881, The Hermitage burned to the ground. Several members of the Burgwin family had been "sitting at the dinner table when the cook suddenly rushed in and announced that the entire roof was one sheet of flame. A large trunk filled with valuables was thrown out of an upper window, and when it struck the ground the lid flew open, a shower of sparks fell in it, and the contents were consumed.

The framing timbers, very large and being of heart pitch pine, stood for many hours after the sides and roof burned away, presenting a very striking appearance as they stood in relief against the sky, erect and in place, a mass of blaze and heat.

This painting was executed by Ralph Johnson Associates, from a sketch made by Eliza Clitherall, John Burgwin's daughter. (Lower Cape Fear Historical Society.)

John Dawson's house once graced the "other corner" at the intersection of Fifth and Market Streets. Located across from the Bellamy Mansion, 502 Market Street boasted the sort of materials a prosperous dry goods merchant could incorporate easily into his own dwelling, including stained glass, rare pink marble fireplaces, and choice timber. The residence of "John Dawson, Esq., . . . will be, when finished, a model of architectural taste and skill," reported the *Wilmington Herald* on November 17, 1857.

About 1823, John Dawson sailed to America from Northern Ireland with his relative, New York's "Merchant Prince" A.T. Stewart. They remained close; Mr. Dawson frequently visited the Stewart Mansion, which was once located on the northwest corner of Fifth Avenue and 34th Street, opposite the Empire State Building. Mr. Dawson was already a successful businessman and a stockholder in the Wilmington and Weldon Railroad when the board of directors suggested he carry a full line of hardware supplies, suitable to build tracks and trestles. His business, located on the northeast corner of Front and Market Streets, soon went full throttle. John Dawson served as mayor of Wilmington during the Civil War.

In 1874, Isaac Grainger's widow, Josie, purchased the house for $7,500. Jean McKoy Graham, a descendant of Isaac Grainger, later moved John Dawson's iron fence to her residence at 201 Forest Hills Drive, where it still stands. A pink marble mantel from the John Dawson House now graces the den of a residence at 218 Forest Hills Drive. (IA1675.)

This deRosset House, on Second Street between Dock and Orange Streets, was the home of Capt. A.L. deRosset of Company B, Sixth Battalion, who was stationed at the Fayetteville Arsenal during the Civil War. Captain deRosset was wounded in several battles and left for dead at Averasboro, but a Federal surgeon saved his life. This photograph was taken *c.* 1940. (1982.46.13.)

The Armand deRosset House, on the northwest corner of Third and Market Streets, was built before the American Revolution. James Sprunt wrote that "with its quaint chimney stacks, it was the Confederate headquarters in our late War Between the States." This photograph was taken c. 1890. (IA3202.)

The north side of Market Street, from Third to Second, consisted of solid buildings, c. 1901. Mrs. Potter's Boarding House is third from the right, with a double porch. At one time, there were as many as 50 boardinghouses in Wilmington; most of them were located in the downtown area. (1981.13.2.)

Mount Lebanon, the home of Judge Joshua Grainger Wright and his bride, Susan Bradley Wright, was built c. 1790. Later, it was the summer home of the Latimer family, descendants of Joshua and Susan Wright, through the Wrights' daughter, Ann Eliza Wright Empie. Mount Lebanon, pictured here in 1958, is gone now, but once stood at the center of what is now Bradley Creek Point. The original name of the tract lives on in Mount Lebanon Chapel. (Lower Cape Fear Historical Society.)

The Wright-Hill-Wootten House, at 11 South Third Street, was constructed well before 1799 when it was damaged by fire. The house was demolished in 1952. North Carolina senator, banker, and physician, John Hill built the house in a style reminiscent of his New England ancestry. His father, a 1754 Harvard graduate, sacrificed some culture for opportunity by moving from Boston to Brunswick County in 1757. (1981.53.2.)

Son John Hill purchased the old Wright plantation in Wrightsboro, "Fairfields," after the American Revolution and gave it to his son William Henry Hill, who happened to be married to the original owner's granddaughter, Ann Wright Claypoole. When their child, Eliza Ann, married William Augustus Wright, the groom took residence in the Hill House and purchased a portion of Fairfields back. Not only were these two families' real estate entwined, so were their genealogies. The marriage of first cousins once removed turned two family trees into a forest, linking, and sometimes strengthening the lines of Captain Thomas Wright, Richard Bradley, Nathaniel Moore, North Carolina Chief Justice Frederick Jones, and Wilmington founder Joshua Grainger.

William Augustus Wright (1807–1878), son of Judge J.G. Wright, lived at least 20 years of his life at 11 South Third Street. The house was located conveniently next to his church, St. James, and across the street from his brother, Dr. Thomas Henry Wright. William Wright was the father of 12 children and Thomas, 11. First cousins must have crossed Third Street continually. As if that were not enough family, Frederick Hill, Eliza Wright's brother and the owner of Orton Plantation, lived with the Wrights after the Civil War. William Wright was president of the Bank of Cape Fear, Wilmington's leading corporate lawyer, and counsel for the Wilmington and Weldon Railroad. When he died on May 14, 1878, a locomotive named for him, the *William A. Wright*, left Wilmington draped in black. During his funeral, which was attended by both whites and African Americans, city hall and the courthouse were closed. Members of the Wright family continued to live in the house at least until 1894.

Like many houses during the 18th and 19th centuries, this one exceeded its bounds and seemed almost to spill into the street. The sidewalk actually wound around the porch, the porch having been there first. A citywide ordinance was adopted in 1874 ordering the removal, after 20 hours' notice, of all piazzas that projected into Market Street, between Second and Ninth Streets. However, as late as 1901, certain dwellings extended into the sidewalk on Fifth Street between Dock and Orange Streets.

Later, distant relatives of William and Eliza Wright occupied the house. When Wright died in 1895, only one of her children had survived. Then the Jewett family, an extended part of the Hill-Wright family tree, took residence here. Eliza Jewett, who married Edward Wootten, lived there from 1903 until 1950.

Like all very old houses, this one had its tales. One story was recalled by James Alfred Locke Miller Jr., brother of author and playwright Anne Russell. Their mother, Leila Wootten, grew up in the house. "Once or twice, in my early 1950s childhood," said Mr. Miller, "I recall adult talk at the old house's dinner table, about how Grandfather's younger sister, Mary Murphy Wootten (1881–1905) announced at the dinner table she did not feel well and she was going up to her fourth floor attic bedroom to die." Miss Wootten then ascended the stairs to her room and died, at the age of 24, on New Year's Eve, 1905. The house was demolished in 1952. (1981.53.2.)

Wilmington merchant and banker James Dawson once lived where the First Union Building now stands, on the northwest corner of Front and Chestnut Streets. The house, built c. 1850 and pictured here c. 1890 (top left), was surrounded by handsome grounds and an elaborate iron fence. As the Civil War was drawing to a close, Mr. Dawson, noting that Confederate currency soon would be play money, purchased all the cotton he could find. Soon after the fall of Fort Fisher, cotton prices soared; he sold his holdings for $300,000, a genuine fortune during Reconstruction. He subsequently founded the Banking House of James Dawson, and established his relative, Isaac Bates Grainger, as cashier.

In 1892, members of the Cape Fear Club, a men's social organization, purchased James Dawson's house. In 1913, the Cape Fear Club moved into a new building on the southeast corner of Second and Chestnut Streets, and James Dawson's house was torn down to make way for the ten-story Murchison Bank Building, now known as the First Union Building. Each of downtown Wilmington's "skyscrapers" sits on former Dawson properties. James Dawson's brother John Dawson once owned the parcel of land on the northeast corner of Front and Market Streets, which is now occupied by the nine-story Atlantic Trust and Banking Company Building.

Pembroke and Sadie Green Jones added their own architectural flair to the entrance of the 1825 Governor Dudley Mansion at 400 South Front Street (bottom right). Residents from 1890 until 1895, they entertained a host of famous and influential guests before a fire damaged portions of the house, forcing them to "refugee" to their home at Airlie. (1980.1.8.)

Thanks to the efforts of preservationists like present owners Connie and Landon Anderson, the 1816 Aaron Lazarus House at 314 Grace Street (bottom left) still exists. The façade, however, is gone. Once the only house on the block, bordered by Third, Grace, Fourth, and Chestnut Streets, it appeared this way c. 1892. (1980.1.8.)

Edward Kidder and his brother Frederick came to Wilmington from Boston in November 1826. They established a shipping business, but Frederick soon returned to Boston. Edward prospered, married Connecticut native Ann Potter, and built a New England-style house at 101 South Third Street, on a double lot that ran all the way from Third to Fourth Street. This photograph was made *c.* 1860. (IA1669.)

Rufus William Hicks and Sallie Spears Hicks built this house at 418 South Third Street in 1889. The 16-room house, constructed from a plan in *Scientific American*, featured granite trim, a slate roof, two Tiffany chandeliers, parquet floors, and many stained-glass windows. From 1935 to 1962 it was the home of D.S. Carr. (Mary Carr Fox.)

Prease Brothers Plumbing and Tinning was located on the south side of Market Street, between Front and Second Streets, next door east to Kelley and Hamlin. William B. McKoy, who was born in this house on December 24, 1852, took this photograph in 1913. (1982.46.37.)

The Robert H. Cowan family lived at 213 North Front Street, but the residence later became an office of the Central Carolina Railroad. The building was torn down in 1910 and replaced with the Bijou Theater. This photograph was taken c. 1880. (1982.46.5.)

The Dr. Thomas Fanning Wood House, located on the northeast corner of Second and Chestnut Streets, had a doctor's office on the first floor and a residence upstairs. In addition to being founder and coeditor of the *North Carolina Medical Journal*, Dr. Wood was also a botanist whose speeches on the subject always drew large crowds. "He dwelt upon the rich flora around Wilmington," wrote one reporter, ". . . the Venus flytraps, the odorous dog-tongue, the modest iris, the mosses, and a thousand other plants that delight the eye and please the senses with their delicate and delicious perfumes."

His son, Dr. Edward Jenner Wood, also practiced here, but lived at 407 South Third Street. This 1943 photograph does not flatter the landscaping, but neighborhood children in the 1930s, like Mary McCarl, used to treasure visits to "Mrs. Jennie's garden." In the 1950s, the Thomas Fanning Wood House was destroyed and the iron fence that surrounded it was moved to a private residence at 2514 Oleander Drive. Belk-Beery, Wilmington's flagship department store of the 1950s, was built in its place. Later, after the store moved to Independence Mall, local government remodeled the building to function as the New Hanover County Public Library. (1994.4.222.)

The Platt K. Dickinson House on the northeast corner of Front and Chestnut Streets was built in 1851. "The elegant residence of P.K. Dickinson, Esq. is now nearly completed, and is especially worthy of notice as evidencing a superior taste in architecture," stated the local paper. In addition to being a director of the Wilmington and Weldon Railroad, Platt Dickinson owned one of seven sawmills in town. All seven could cut more than 140,000 feet of timber and turn out 100,000 feet of lumber daily.

Pembroke Jones, the most famous occupant of this house, was three months old when his mother, Jane Lord Jones, died in 1859. Pembroke Jones's maternal aunt, Mrs. Alice Lord Platt Dickinson, raised her nephew, whose father, a Navy officer, was often away on military duty. Mr. and Mrs. Platt Dickinson had no children of their own, and when they died, they bequeathed their estate to Pembroke Jones. With his inheritance, he entered the rice milling business. He named his first child, who died at age five, Alice Dickinson Jones.

The house was demolished in 1900 to make way for the three-story Murchison Bank Building, which still sits at 200 North Front Street. (IA499.)

Young Mary Borden Wallace sits in front of the family home at 419 North Third Street, c. 1914. Behind her, the handsome houses in the 300 block of Red Cross Street attest to the beauty of the old neighborhood. (Lower Cape Fear Historical Society.)

A pioneer in local education, legendary teacher Amy Bradley lived in a "Little Brown Cottage" on the grounds of Tileston School, pictured in this 1884 photograph. Both the cottage's interior decoration and the surrounding garden were as ordered as her lessons. Wilmington writer Diane Cobb Cashman recorded in her book, *Headstrong, The Biography of Amy Morris Bradley*, "Pupils were allowed to enjoy the flowers, but not to touch them. The lawn was considered 'as sacred as the Holy City.' " Coincidentally, Miss Bradley's lawn is now owned by the Roman Catholic Church, which utilizes the old Tileston School building as a parochial school. (IA185.)

The William H. Sprunt House at 223 North Third Street was built c. 1900. The formal areas were on the first floor, five bedrooms on the second, and a workshop and a room used occasionally for skating on the third floor. William Sprunt, the youngest brother of philanthropist James Sprunt, contributed generously to St. Andrew's Presbyterian Church and donated a wing to James Walker Hospital to be used for the care of black patients and as a nurses' dormitory. (IA1684.)

In 1885, Robert Rankin Bellamy opened a drugstore on the northwest corner of Front and Market Streets, where he sold primarily wholesale medicines and marketed "double distilled extracts for the ladies." In 1895, he built this house at 509 Market Street, next door to his parents' home, the Bellamy Mansion. The Robert R. Bellamy House burned in the early 1980s. (I.J. Isaacs. *Wilmington Up to Date*, 1902.) (IA1544.)

When architect and builder James F. Post died in 1899, it was noted that "among the more notable structures he designed and in most instances built were the city hall and opera house, the splendid Bellamy Mansion on Fifth and Market streets (and) the William A. Wright residence on Sixth and Market streets, many years the residence of Mr. George Harriss and lately purchased by Congressman-elect John D. Bellamy . . ."

William A. Wright lived here briefly before moving to 11 South Third Street, where he would live until his death in 1878. His brother Joshua G. Wright resided and practiced law at 602 Market Street from the mid-1850s until 1863. According to James Post's ledgers housed in the Lower Cape Fear Historical Society archives, the architect did additional work on the house in 1858, the year the Wrights installed a lavish oak and copper bathtub, the first in the state. Joshua Grainger Wright died in 1863, and his wife, Mary, in 1865. In 1869, their heirs sold 602 Market Street to George Harriss (1827–1899), owner of George Harriss and Company, a ship brokerage firm located at 109 North Water Street. (North Carolina Collection, University of North Carolina Library at Chapel Hill.)

Attorney John D. Bellamy purchased the Wright-Harriss House in 1899 and hired architect Charles McMillen to alter it. The proposed changes were so immense that the local newspaper took note. "Both the interior and exterior decorations will be on an elaborate scale, but those on the interior will be probably unsurpassed in the whole state. Mahogany, cherry and oak, carved from the solid, will be used in profusion in the stair work, mantels and the main newel post will be carved in acanthus leaves," reported the *Dispatch*, September 14, 1899.

New York decorators Duryea and Potter iced the architectural cake with a host of rich effects including stained glass, ivory woodwork, silk wallcovering, an onyx fireplace, 15th-century wainscoting, exotic tapestries, and tile mosaics. Soon many Wilmingtonians were calling Congressman Bellamy's house "The Bellamy Mansion," which must have been confusing with the original only a block away.

John D. Bellamy, a close friend of President Woodrow Wilson, entertained often and lavishly in the third-floor ballroom. The house finally was owned by his granddaughter, Emma Bellamy Williamson Hendren. The Wright-Harriss-Bellamy House burned in August 1972 and was demolished in July 1973. The front door was salvaged and installed at the Philly Deli restaurant at Hanover Center. Several interior railings were incorporated into the decor of Annabelle's Restaurant. (IA4949.)

Wilmington merchant Abram David built the house at 619 Market Street, which he later sold to Benjamin H.J. Ahrens. Mr. Ahrens also built two commercial buildings that still stand, one at 110–112 Market Street, the other at 31 South Front Street. Pictured here, c. 1906, is Jake Solomon, who lived across the street at 616 Market. The chimney pots from the Ahrens House are now part of the James Moss Burns Jr. residence at 1417 Hawthorne Road. (1992.31.370.)

In 1902, Abram David moved next door, to this new house designed by architect Charles McMillen. Later, 617 Market Street was the home of George H. Hutaff, who purchased a Coca-Cola franchise that covered eastern North Carolina and parts of Virginia and South Carolina in 1902. Mr. Hutaff's daughter, Tabitha Hutaff McEachern, is a longtime local history enthusiast and generous patron of the arts.

In the 1920s, James Sprunt said the house that used to sit on the southwest corner of Fifth and Orange streets was "very likely more nearly now what it was one hundred years ago than any other residence in the city." Once the home of the Reverend Daniel Morrelle and Thomas F. Davis, the house took its name from its most famous owner, General Alexander MacRae, president of the Wilmington and Manchester Railroad and the father of nine sons, including Donald, father of Hugh MacRae. Alexander MacRae moved to the remote Fifth, or "Boundary" Street, c. 1840, after fire damaged "Dunnegan Castle," his home on the southeast corner of Front and Princess Streets. Though often called away, the father and eight surviving sons made this house home base during the Civil War. Letters sent to and from 420 Orange Street shortly after the war paint a fascinating picture of Wilmington at the time and of ambitious young men able to envision large-scale business opportunities despite hard times. One of Alexander's sons continued to live at 420 Orange Street until his death on December 14, 1928. Though a railroad official, Walter Gwyn MacRae was perhaps more famous for reciting complete newspaper articles after just one hearing. A wooden room, a portion of which can be seen in the photograph, adjoined General MacRae's kitchen. It was home to the "Queen of Mondigo," a slave who received special privileges in the MacRae household. (1982.46.49.)

Designed by James F. Post, the Wood-MacRae House at 713 Market Street was built for John Coffin Wood in 1853. Donald MacRae, son of General Alexander MacRae, purchased it in 1859 and immediately tried to make it reflect his Scottish heritage. "One cannot fail to be attracted by the beautiful appearance of the dwelling of Donald MacRae on Market Street, since the process of rough casting and painting has been affected. It is built in a singular style of architecture, presents a castellated appearance—one which we admire greatly—and taken as a whole may now be reckoned one of the finest houses in the place, and an ornament to the street," reported the *Daily Herald*, March 2, 1860. (Calder Collection.)

During the Civil War, Donald moved his family to Carbonton, where he mined iron ore and farmed. His son, Hugh, was born in Carbonton in 1865. Yankees commandeered the MacRae home in Wilmington and set up a makeshift hospital. After the war ended and the Yankees went home, Donald MacRae remained in Carbonton until 1867, minding his mine of iron ore. As always, the house attracted attention. "General Robert Ransom has been inquiring about your house, wanting to know if you will rent it and the price if you will rent it," wrote Alexander MacRae to Donald in 1866. A few months later, brothers Billy (Gen. William MacRae) and Walter moved into the castle as caretakers.

"Billy leaves for New York tomorrow, I think to attend a railroad convention. Walter has been using an alarm clock to wake him up since he moved to your house, and says that the only trouble about it is that he sits up half the night to see that it strikes at the right time," reported Roderick on his brother, the battle strategist and future railroad executive whose excessive efficiency occasionally drove his siblings wild. Once, while living in the castle, Gen. William MacRae, with Walter's assistance, made an intricate drawing for owner Donald, "showing how the cows and Yankees have destroyed all the fruit trees, leaving nothing but the stumps thereof." In 1892, Donald's son Hugh MacRae had inherited the castle. Ten years later, he asked his Tileston school friend, architect Henry Bacon, to remodel his home. Bacon, whose most famous work would be the Lincoln Memorial, preferred public and commercial design. Other than "Chesterwood," located in Stockton, Massachusetts, Bacon's sole residential work was for the MacRae family of Wilmington.

Henry Bacon added Tudor baronial features in keeping with Mr. MacRae's Scottish heritage, which the owner took seriously. A branch of the family that once occupied Scotland's Eileen Donan Castle, Wilmington's MacRaes ate haggis well into the 19th century. Frank Bacon, the architect's brother and an internationally known archaeologist and furniture designer, served as interior decorator for the castle. Though some of the furniture has survived, the house was destroyed in 1955; 18-inch walls turned to dust.

Coordinated landscaping enhanced the rear lawns of the Hugh MacRae House, on the left, and the Agnes MacRae Parsley House, on the right. Mr. MacRae and Mrs. Parsley, who were also brother and sister, apparently employed the same gardeners for both yards, which ran through to Princess Street. The Parsley stable, a 1906 English-style, two-story structure designed by Henry Bonitz, can be glimpsed on the right. It was built of Borden brick, and had limestone trim and a slate roof. (1988.60.1.)

The 711 Market Street residence of Walter Parsley and Agnes MacRae was built in 1886. On December 8, 1897, the Parsleys' five-year-old son, Walter L. Parsley Jr., described as "manly and very bright," ran out into Market Street during a game of chase. He was hit by a bicycle and died a few hours later. After the accident, his grief stricken parents spent more time at their home on Masonboro Sound. They later built a grander house, Live Oaks, which was designed by architect Henry Bacon.

Henry E. Bonitz was the architect for this house at 719 Market Street, which was owned by Elizabeth Hashagen Vollers, widow of Luhr Vollers. Built on the northwest corner at Eighth Street in 1904, it completed an impressive block already occupied by the Solomon, Parsley-Kuck, and MacRae houses. Though the house burned, the impressive Vollers Mausoleum at Oakdale Cemetery endures. (1993.11.73.)

The home of John H. Rehder and his wife, Elise Bissinger Rehder, was located on the northeast corner of Eighth and Market Streets. From the turret, Elise could see the two homes she lived in as a girl. Elise and John Rehder spent their free time traveling to Europe, where they collected many elements of their personal dream house, as well as chose distinctive items to market among the usual at J.H. Rehder and Company. They chose Murano glass in Europe to embellish their house, a pink-and-green glass chandelier in Venice for their dining room, and their bedroom furniture in Paris. As jovial hosts, the Rehders entertained frequently. Guests at their annual New Year's Eve party could dance to the music of an orchestra in the third floor ballroom, descend to the second floor to play billiards in the handsome game room, which was fitted with bleachers, or just relax in the baronial parlor surrounded by Mr. Rehder's medieval armor collection. Handsome grounds and a first-floor greenhouse seemed natural, considering that Mr. Rehder was brother to Will, North Carolina's oldest florist.

Wilmington writer Barbara Marcroft, who spent time in the Rehder home, remembered the elegance and convenience. "The front door was beautiful and very heavy. There was silk paper on the walls, Venetian glass everywhere. On the landing, halfway up the staircase, there was a lighted wrought iron statue. The Rehders had an intercom system. They also had a button on the dining room wall that swung the wall around to reveal a full liquor cabinet. Additionally, there was a button beside their bed that unlocked their back door. They could let the help in without getting out of bed."

Mrs. Marcroft also took note of Mrs. Rehder's stories."When President Taft came to town, John and Elise Rehder were official hosts to his male secretary. John Rehder took the male secretary down to Airlie to see his close friend Pembroke Jones. When they got there, Mr. Jones greeted them.

"Noting that no one else was home, John Rehder asked, 'Where is everybody?'

"'Ah, hell, they've all gone downtown to see President Taft,' Pembroke Jones answered, inviting them into the dining room for champagne. The bottle exploded as he opened it, covering a red velvet tablecloth with bubbles and glass. Undaunted, Jones grabbed the whole thing and threw it in the fireplace.

"Once, in the early 1920s, when the Rehders returned from a big trip, they invited niece Jessie and nephew Henry over to pick a present out from a large pile of gifts. They were just children, but Jessie, the future novelist, chose a sword. Henry, who would one day be a major local art collector, chose a painting.

"The Sadgwars lived at 15 North Eighth Street. Sometimes, on warm nights when the windows were open, we could hear one of the Sadgwar sisters playing the piano. It was beautiful." (1992.78.48.)

The Luhr Vollers House used to occupy the northwest corner of Second and Orange Streets, where the U.S.O. building stands today. A native of Hannover, Germany, Vollers was a businessman. His nephew, Louis H. Vollers, was a builder who constructed many houses and commercial buildings, including the Southern Bell Telephone and Telegraph Company building at 121–129 Princess Street. This photograph was taken c. 1900. (1983.20.2.)

In 1907, architect Burrett Stephens built the Prairie-style house on the left at 1709 Market Street for Ella Weil. It contained ten rooms and featured solid bronze fixtures, mahogany mantels, and oak parquet floors. Two mansions, the Holt-Wise House (on right) and the Emerson-Kenan House, built in 1908, sandwiched the smaller house. It was demolished, perhaps mercifully, in the 1970s. (Calder Collection.)

John Cowan Bowden and his wife, Emily Jane Tilley Bowden, lived on the northwest corner of Second and Chestnut Streets, where the Cape Fear Hotel now stands. The house was built c. 1840 and existed until 1924. John Bowden was a naval stores inspector. The Roger Moore family lived in the house next door. In 1923, the Cape Fear Hotel replaced both houses. (Louis T. Moore Collection, New Hanover County Library.)

The Matt Heyer family lived at 420 North Second Street from 1854 until 1967. Mr. Heyer owned the Southern Building. His son, Henry, was an attorney, vice-president of the Meares Harriss Printing Company, and treasurer of Spirittine Chemical. (IA 1661.)

Merchant Samuel Bear and his wife, Barbara, lived here at 311 North Front Street. After Samuel's death, Barbara moved to a new house, designed in 1905 by architect Charles McMillen, on the southeast corner of Fifth and Chestnut Streets. In 1913, the Bear family replaced the house on North Front Street with a large commercial building. (IA1658.)

Emmanuel Israel Bear was born the day the Temple of Israel was consecrated, May 12, 1876. This c. 1930 photograph shows E.I. Bear's residence at 114 North Fifth Street, near the southeast corner of Fifth and Chestnut Streets, next door to Barbara Bear's home. (1985.72.1.)

The Lucile Sternberger Goldburg House at 112 North Fifth Street was designed by Henry Bonitz and built by Louis H. Vollers. It was dressed in its winter best, February 25, 1942, after a 7-inch snowfall stunned the city. (1985.72.34.)

Once the residence of F.A. Thompson, the house at 109 North Fifth Street had been sold and converted into apartments by 1942. A housing shortage during World War II led to many such makeovers. A BellSouth building now occupies this spot. (1985.72.45.)

Houses just north of the city hall formed a no-nonsense background to this 1928 Louis T. Moore photograph of the Feast of Pirates parade, photographed by Louis T. Moore. On the left, a Buccaneer lurks in front of the residence of J.J. Joyner. The house on the right served as headquarters for the North Carolina Sorosis. (IA64.)

The Swann-Weathers House at 117 North Third Street was disassembled in 1922 and moved to 1405 Airlie Road, where it was rebuilt. Descendants of C.M. Weathers, Robert McCarl, James McCarl, and Mary M. Wilson still own the house. The property on the southwest corner of Third and Chestnut Streets became part of MacMillan and Cameron.

Ear, nose, and throat specialist Dr. J.G. Murphy built the house at 115 South Third Street. Dr. Murphy, a member of the nearby First Presbyterian Church, was also Sunday school superintendent of the Queen Street Mission, a black church. The Murphy house was owned later by Mrs. Herbert King. She advertised rooms for rent with this 1948 postcard reading, "Guest home. Modern, heated." (1995.81.4.)

In 1932, artist Claude Howell sketched the Rankin-Wright-Strange House, located at 206 South Front Street, shortly before the building was destroyed. The chimneys of the Smith-Anderson House can be seen on the right. (Private collection.)

As late as the 1920s, Greenville Sound was touted as medicinal, therapeutic, and sure to be appreciated. "A healthful and comfortable location where you can have your chickens, cow and garden. Twenty minutes from the city on a splendid road," advertised real estate broker Thomas H. Wright. "Save doctor bills and have fresh air, health and comfort in a home that will steadily increase in value as water frontage is taken up."

The house that came to be known as Monk Barns, which was built on the south end of Greenville Sound c. 1754, was designed to capitalize on the fresh air. The distinguishing feature of the three-story house was a crenellated tower used by residents to cool off on hot summer

nights and by Confederates to monitor blockade running. Dr. William A. Berry, a Wilmington physician, purchased Monk Barns in 1852. The house's moniker came from a Sir Walter Scott novel Dr. Berry and his daughter, Mrs. William H. McKoy, read entitled *The Antiquary*. In it, there is a place known as "Monkbarns, a solitary old house, built with a contempt for architectural regularity that commanded a fine prospect of bay and shipping." Despite the air of antiquity, the first telephone line in North Carolina was installed in 1878 from Monk Barns to Dr. Berry's town home at 11 South Fifth Street. (IA178.)

Dr. Edwin Anderson, who also lived in the Smith-Anderson House at 102 Orange Street, spent summers at Eshcol, his home on Masonboro Sound. His son Edwin was born here in 1860 and grew up to be an admiral in the U.S. Navy and a celebrated war hero. He received many honors for his service in the Spanish-American War, World War I, the Boxer Rebellion, and his command of the Asiatic fleet. Eshcol was razed in 1963. (1995.109.17.)

Just as Dr. Anderson had a medical office next to his house at 102 Orange Street, he also maintained one at Masonboro Sound next to Eshcol. However, his office hours were limited; Dr. Anderson was also a businessman with interests in sawmills, drygoods, and a turpentine distillery. Though the office survived, it has been moved to 7520 Masonboro Sound Road and is now a private residence. The Anderson photographs were made *c.* 1880. (1995.109.13.)

These cabins were occupied by Dr. Anderson's servants. When his son, Admiral Edwin Anderson, retired to Eshcol in 1924, he had another house custom-built for his longtime Japanese servant, Sito. Unfortunately, Sito was detained on a visit to Japan and never occupied his soundfront home. (1995.109.15.)

Captain Thomas Wright built Finian in 1765 on land owned by his wife's family, the Graingers. It was home to Solomon's Lodge, a Masonic group that met on Masonboro Sound in the 18th century. In 1773, William Hooper, a signer of the Declaration of Independence, purchased Finian for 150 pounds. Owned later by the Parsley and Peschau families, Finian burned to the ground on March 17, 1931. (Lower Cape Fear Historical Society.)

Pembroke Jones (1858–1919), a Wilmington native and a wealthy rice planter and mill owner, purchased a 3,000-acre tract of land north of Summer Rest Road through his cousin, real estate broker Thomas H. Wright, c. 1902. Mr. Jones called the tract "Pembroke Park at Airlie," and constructed a 28-mile shell road through it. Though he gave his wife free reign at Airlie, their other soundfront Wilmington home, Pembroke Park was his playground. In contrast to the sea of flowers at Airlie, Pembroke Park had not one cultivated blossom. The woods were Mr. Jones's delight. He shared their bounteous game with distinguished friends who left their own palatial quarters both to be regaled royally by their flamboyant host and to affect the need to hunt.

Though Pembroke Jones originally planned to build a much plainer house, he was challenged by a friend who happened to be an architect. "You are losing a great opportunity for getting something just a little more expensive but ever so much more beautiful," said J. Stewart Barney, who proceeded to build Pembroke Jones an Italianate showplace in which the doorknobs alone cost more than the owner's original plan. The Italian ambassador himself visited Pembroke Park and declared the new house "the most perfect note of Italy in America."

Though many Wilmingtonians called it the "Lodge," Mr. Jones often referred to his 1908 getaway, located on what is now Great Oak Drive, as the "Bungalow." The house had three adjoining great rooms with multi-vaulted ceilings, many elaborately furnished apartments in one wing, and a kitchen fit to cater many guests in the other. The great hall sported two large Italian Renaissance stone mantels, which were each supported by two large female nudes. The walls of the apartments were divided into panels by Ionic columns in bas-relief. The furnishings, which included many large painted chests, had once adorned an Italian palace.

According to Lewis Philip Hall, author of *Land of the Golden River*, the kitchen was large enough to contain a complete bakery and the butler's pantry held a "gold and silver service for two hundred." A trapdoor led to a wine cellar. The ceiling of the immense dining room was solid and vaulted, but natural light often bathed the room from an adjoining solarium that featured a glass ceiling, augmented throughout with fine black wire. One evening, the after-dinner entertainment was a private concert by Enrico Caruso. Caruso's pianist was ill, so Pembroke Jones engaged Mildred Kornegay, a pianist at the Bijou Theater, to accompany the world-famous tenor.

Outside, facing Wrightsville Sound, an old Gatling gun was mounted on the terrace, close to a stone lily pool. A bridge nearby matched the Bungalow. Between the house and Wrightsville Sound, in the midst of a grove of oaks, pines, and magnolias, there was an imposing bronze statue of Cupid. Beyond the terraced lawn, on the opposite side of the house, sat the Temple of Love, which was designed by John Russell Pope, Pembroke and Sadie Jones' son-in-law. Mr. Pope was also the architect for a series of buildings spun from this design that culminated in his most famous American creation: the Jefferson Memorial. A coquina gazebo, the centerpiece of the Jones' temple, canopied a small fountain ornamented by a bronze reproduction of Andrea del Verrocchio's 1470 Florentine sculpture, *Putto with Dolphin*. The six-columned gazebo was surrounded by a circle made of four wedge-shaped pools that were connected by walkways. Each pool held a different kind of fish. The pools also were made of coquina, created by mixing concrete with shells from Wrightsville Sound. In 1915, architect Samuel Howe wrote, "Of course, the temple is white, but not the white of Italy's statuary marble nor the polished equivalent from some neighboring state, but following the precedent of the great craft workers of the Renaissance, local materials have been exclusively used. Here is the oldest and newest form of building material."

Though mostly unoccupied after Pembroke Jones's death in 1919, the Bungalow stood until 1955, when it burned. During the 35-year period, more than a few young Wilmingtonians proved their bravery by wandering through the moonlit little palace while the watchman looked the other way. More sinister visitors came, too, and, over the years, many of the handsome Tuscan furnishings vanished, the artwork disappeared, and even the tile floors were hauled away. In 1982, bulldozers pulverized shards of leaded glass, red tile, and polished stone as they graded Pembroke Park, transforming what had been home to one family into the immense subdivision known now as Landfall. All that remains on the original site are the stark gazebo and the gates that John Russell Pope designed; these have now been incorporated in the Lion's Gate complex. The balustrade from the lodge was salvaged after the 1955 fire and added into adjacent homes at 530 and 532 Waynick Boulevard at Wrightsville Beach, the James Moss Burns Jr. House, and the Miriam Burns Stokes House. (Henry Bacon McKoy Collection.)

In addition to Pembroke Park, Pembroke and Sadie Green Jones also owned Airlie, the land which was once known as "Mount Lebanon." Just as Pembroke reveled in life at the Lodge, Sadie considered Airlie her home. Even before the Joneses were married, she owned a "fishing shack" there known as the Seaside Park Hotel. After their marriage, she began both to refine and enlarge the building. By 1916, a visiting architect wrote, "Additions have been made and wings thrown out here and there until it is a house of many mansions. The roofs of Airlie, with their many angles and corners, suggest all manner of surprises and ramblings, and the interior does not belie the promise. You never get to the end of such a house. There is always a new room, or a passage leading to unknown territory. One might live there for a week and never guess that there was a covered tennis court right in the middle of the house just off the breakfast room."

The "new rooms" eventually included a ballroom, a banquet hall, and 38 apartments for guests. It all came in handy in the fall of 1912, when the Joneses' only daughter, Sadie, married John Russell Pope. Five hundred guests descended on Airlie for a wedding deemed, "one of the most elaborate and brilliant . . . ever held in this part of the State." The bride and groom greeted friends under a canopy of white roses in the dining room at Airlie while a New York caterer served food and drink among the smilax garlands on the indoor tennis court.

The appointments throughout the house were stunning. Eighteenth-century heirlooms from Mrs. Jones's family, General Thomas Jefferson Green, and his descendants were scattered among European treasures. Many local children, invited to the annual Christmas party at Airlie, returned home with expensive and unique gifts, ranging anywhere from jeweled watches to miniature Mark Cross tool sets.

Though much has been said through the years about "keeping up with the (Pembroke) Joneses," there was more to attract their friends to Pembroke Park and Airlie than luxurious surroundings. Though surviving photographs depict somber guests, humor abounded. Minnie Evans (1893–1987) and her husband, Julius, worked for Pembroke Jones. Though she grew famous as an artist, Mrs. Evans worked as the gatekeeper; her husband worked in the garden. She once told local writer Barbara Marcroft, "I remember people coming and going in carriages to Mr. Jones's parties. There was laughter, so much laughter, and sometimes they would sing beautifully," she said.

Pembroke Jones died in 1919, and three years later, Sadie married their close friend, railroad executive and art lover Henry Walters.

Greensboro photographer Charles Farrell took these pictures in the mid-1930s, when he accompanied author E.T.H. Shaffer to the Lodge and Airlie. Their work was published in *Carolina Gardens*. (North Carolina Division of Archives and History.)

W.A. Corbett purchased Airlie on January 16, 1948, for $150,000. The Corbett family moved into the rambling house, which provided a maze of museum-quality materials and a hide-and-seek heaven for their grandchildren. The wallpaper, pictured here, was painted for Sadie Walters by a visiting Chinese artist.

Corbett family dinners at Airlie were centered around a dining room table made of a single piece of mahogany. When the house was razed in the 1950s, Mr. Corbett donated the table to Wilmington College; it is still utilized by the University of North Carolina at Wilmington. Waddell's son Wilbur Corbett bought the chandelier in England.

Two

Cape Fear Foundations

Churches, clubs, government buildings, and hospitals form a solid base for life along the Cape Fear River, but no matter how sacred or exclusive the buildings, consuming fires and common demolition tools took their toll.

What architectural treasure did this ancient buttressed wall support? During a demolition in the 1960s, excavation exposed it sitting in the center of the block bordered by Chestnut, Princess, Water, and Front Streets. According to local researcher William M. Reaves, in Wilmington's earliest days, Water Street did not exist except as marsh. Front Street was considered too wet for stable construction without massive supports like the ones seen here. Logs, ballast stones, and courses of brick were placed periodically along the riverbank, only to sink beneath the mud. In time, subterranean tunnels and tons of matter made Water Street suitable on which to build and made Front Street solid. (1982.46.102.)

"The Custom House is a new and elegant building . . . stowed away in a cranny almost out of sight," wrote a visitor to Wilmington, c. 1845. Indeed, a customhouse existed on this cramped site as early as 1819, but as historian Henry Bacon McKoy stated, "This original building was destroyed by fire on Jan. 17, 1840, which has been the fate of most of the private and public buildings of the town, unless demolished by foolish men and officials." Government agents purchased adjoining property and, in 1843, contracted New York architect John Norris to build a finer and larger customhouse.

A year later, this dignified three-story Greek Revival-style building stood on Water Street, as a handsome symbol of Wilmington's growing importance as a port city. Built primarily of Connecticut red sandstone and Baltimore pressed brick, the doors and window shutters were made of heavy wrought iron and the roof of thick copper, plated with tin. The Tower of the Winds column capitals shown here were the first example of this form in Wilmington. Until 1874, the Custom House also served as a U.S. post office. In 1915, the venerable building and every other structure on the east side of Water Street between Market and Princess Streets were razed to make way for the present custom house. Lamps from the building now grace the North Front Street entrance to the Cotton Exchange.

This newly discovered image dates from c. 1908 and was probably taken by photographer Eric Norden. The 1899 Masonic Temple at 17 North Front Street looms in the background. (Calder Collection.)

According to Dr. Chris Fonvielle, author of *The Wilmington Campaign*, the Cape Fear Minute Men took possession of Fort Johnston at Southport in January 1861. Five years after the United States repossessed the fort, c. 1870, this "new" hospital emerged. It was sold in 1888, moved to 413 East Bay Street, and was used as a private residence. (North Carolina Division of Archives and History.)

The original structure at Fort Caswell took 12 years to build and was completed in 1838. The fort consisted of a citadel whose three entrances were each fortified with two caponniers, like the one seen here. Flared slits in the 3-foot-thick masonry walls provided a 36 degree shooting range from within while allowing only 1 degree of exposure to incoming ammunition. The entire complex, surrounded by a creek-fed moat, had a bridge that could be raised to function as the fort's massive door. (1976.55.49.)

The 1849 Price's Creek Lighthouse at Southport was part of the Brunswick County beacon system that included lights at Bald Head Island, Oak Island, Upper Jetty, and Orton Point. The shell of this lighthouse remains. (1981.71.15.)

This was not the first Federal Point lighthouse at Fort Fisher. An 1837 beacon, 30 feet high and made of brick, was dismantled during the Civil War. This one was built in 1866, not long before this photograph was taken. The mounds of Fort Fisher are visible, still intact and lacking vegetation. The lighthouse, used only until 1879, was destroyed by fire sometime after 1925. (1962.44.14.)

In the late 1940s, the foot of Grace Street was still home to the Atlantic Fireboat House, and businesses filled the block. From this vantage-point today, the Cotton Exchange parking lot is on the right, the parking deck is on the left, and the Hilton Hotel has replaced the fireboat house. (1994.4.142.)

Hugh Morton photographed the *Frying Pan* lightship, which was replaced in 1964 by a platform, c. 1950. While on the trip for taking this photograph, Mr. Morton and pilot Colonel Ben Washburn were driven south by strong winds and had barely enough fuel to make it back to Carl Dunn's airport, now long replaced by Independence Mall. (1999.29.1.)

In the latter half of the 19th century, the riverfront was not the scenic, placid place we see today. It was a teeming residential and commercial district. At the time, the post office was still located in the old customhouse on Water Street. Heavy commercial river traffic, busy warehouses, serious drainage problems, and assorted port-related business made waterfront activities hard on the faint of heart. "In the selection of a site for the new post office, we hope a due regard to the welfare of the ladies will be observed. A central location removed from the bustle and filth of Water Street will be more appropriate and equally convenient to our business community," reported the Evening Post, January 29, 1873.

The cornerstone was laid at 152 North Front Street on June 4, 1889. W.A. Freret, supervising architect of the U.S. Treasury, designed Wilmington's 1889–91 post office, a massive Romanesque structure made of Wadesboro, North Carolina brownstone. Earlier, Freret had designed an exotic building that still stands at 622 Canal Street in New Orleans, using Solomonic columns similar to those in the Wilmington Post Office. James F. Post served as supervising architect and William F. Smith as contractor. Two faces sculpted of concrete peered out from the wall, one smiling and one frowning, to represent the emotions mail can bring. Elaborate lighting fixtures from Philadelphia and large cherry roll-top desks from Baltimore warmed the interior decor.

The old post office was a good corporate customer for local businesses, both big and small. Early records indicate that J.A. Springer supplied 80 tons of anthracite egg coal, William E. Worth & Company provided 25,000 pounds of ice, and H. Watson received $11.50 in 1897 for a dozen etched glass globes and 24 porcelain ones. Local businessmen John MacRae, J.W. Murchison, and John Hanby usually supervised the building's repairs and requisitions. The local weather bureau, located on the roof of the post office, was a special maintenance problem, since it was partially exposed to the elements it monitored.

After months of conflict among preservationists, politicians, and a local labor union, the old post office was demolished in 1936 after standing less than 50 years. The stone building was so sturdy and well built that it was extremely difficult to raze, giving the large temporary labor force plenty to do. Scant pieces of the building remain; the finials have been incorporated into the landscape at a Live Oak Parkway residence and the clock resides in the basement of Cape Fear Museum. Sipke Feenstra purchased stones from the building and used them to pave the end of the Old Wrightsboro Road. In 1942, the airport expanded and runway now covers that part of the old post office.

It was replaced on the site by the present post office, a brick Neoclassical Revival-style structure alleged to have been inspired by John Norris's 1840s customhouse. Once again, a stone building, stronger than the three pigs' straw, wood, or brick, had been dismantled with great difficulty to supplant one of lesser strength and, many would argue, of lesser beauty.

This photograph was taken May 25, 1936, from the vantage point of the Murchison Building, known now as the First Union Building. (United States Postal Service, Postmaster Walter Hunt.)

The Woodrow Wilson Hut, Wilmington headquarters for the American Legion, was razed shortly before demolition of the post office in 1936. In 1920, when this photograph was taken, it was not only patriotic to name something after the president, it was a matter of civic pride. Woodrow Wilson's father, the Reverend Joseph R. Wilson, was minister of First Presbyterian Church from 1874 until 1885. (1987.23.27.)

Though construction began on the first St. James Church in 1753, meager funds delayed completion until about 1769. The building sat between Third and Fourth Streets and jutted out into Market Street. After 70 years, space and aesthetics called for a new building, but members recycled what they could of the old one. "Proposals will be received by the undersigned for pulling down the Episcopal Church in this place, and cleaning the brick," announced vestrymen Thomas H. Wright and W.C. Lord on February 1, 1839. The Gothic Revival-style building that replaced it still stands on the southeast corner of Third and Market Streets.

In 1890, when locals heard evangelist Sam Jones was coming to town, they built the Sam Jones Tabernacle, at Seventh and Campbell Streets, to accommodate the crowd. His sermons, Bible lessons peppered with humor, were so popular that the *Wilmington Messenger* printed them verbatim. (1984.70.8.)

Mary Bridgers was the daughter of Colonel Rufus R. Bridgers, president of the Wilmington and Weldon Railroad and the Carolina and Augusta Railroad. Miss Bridgers, who once owned 22 acres of Carolina Heights, was fascinated with architecture and with the Christian Science movement. Her two main interests intersected in the construction of the First Church of Christ Scientist on her property in 1907. The building later was purchased by Temple Baptist Church. The Bluethenthal House on the right still stands. (1988.65.13.)

Builders John C. and Robert B. Wood built Front Street Methodist Church in 1844, according to the Greek Revival-style plans of architect James F. Post. The church, located on the northeast corner of Front and Walnut Streets, was unique for that period of time, as its congregation was fully integrated. It burned February 21, 1886, when fire spread from a docking steamship to level seven blocks of downtown Wilmington. (IA165.)

The congregation of Front Street Methodist Church rebuilt in 1886, but chose a site farther from the river, on the northeast corner of Fourth and Mulberry Streets. This time, they let scripture rather than geography lead them to a name—Grace Methodist Church. Eventually, Mulberry Street took the name of the church. Nevertheless, the congregation once again lost its building to fire in 1947. This 1902 photograph is used by permission of the North Carolina Division of Archives and History. (IA1551.)

Fifth Street Methodist Episcopal Church, located on the east side between Nun and Church Streets, was organized in 1847 by members of the Front Street Methodist Church who felt the south side needed its own building. Miles Costin donated land for the 1848 church, pictured here c. 1884. By 1888, the congregation had outgrown its building; it was destroyed to make space for the "new" Fifth Avenue Methodist Church, which still stands. (IA232.)

By 1851, the congregation of St. James Church already had outgrown its new building. Though too small for its needs, it was also too aesthetically pleasing to alter. As a young member of the church, as Magdalene deRosset lay dying, she made one last request of her father, Senior Warden Armand J. deRosset. "Give my portion of your estate toward the purchase of a lot for the new church," she asked.

After Magdalene's death, Dr. deRosset bought a lot on the northeast corner of Third and Red Cross Streets, a location considered promising because of its proximity to the Wilmington and Weldon Railroad. St. James supplied $15,000 in building funds. The Reverend Dr. R.B. Drane, rector of St. James, chose the name St. John's because James and John, two of Jesus' disciples, were brothers, and Dr. Drane wanted brotherly love to exist between the two churches. Work began on St. John's on November 21, 1853, when Bishop Thomas Atkinson, Dr. Drane, and a contingent from the mother church processed from St. James to the new construction site for a cornerstone ceremony.

During the Civil War, St. John's and St. James were ordered to pray for the president of the United States. As both churches planned to pray instead for "those in rightful authority," the keys were confiscated and the churches closed until prayers were offered for Abraham Lincoln. This photograph was taken c. 1880. (1982. 46.16.)

First Presbyterian Church.   WILMINGTON, N. C.

The original First Presbyterian Church building, erected in 1818 on South Front Street, was small; its quick and fiery end the following year was thought by some strident souls to be due justice since some of the building funds resulted from a lottery. The second, built in 1820 on the east side of Front Street between Orange and Dock, was grander, featuring box pews and an ornamented pulpit perched above Ionic columns. In May 1858, St. Paul's Lutheran Church organized at the First Presbyterian Church.

   Sadly, the second First Presbyterian Church building burned as well. An assembly hall on Marcus (Church Alley) was all that was left after a fire on April 13, 1859. Later, the Wilmington Hebrew Congregation worshipped in the assembly hall prior to 1876, when the Temple of Israel was dedicated. The building was destroyed c. 1950.

After the second building burned, church members voted to move away from the fanning winds off the Cape Fear River. They chose the present location on the northeast corner of Third and Orange Streets. Samuel Sloan from Philadelphia designed the building pictured on the previous page, Wilmington's First Baptist Church, and the Bank of New Hanover. He was also responsible for many of the state's important buildings, including the Executive Mansion in Raleigh, the Western Insane Asylum in Morganton, and the original memorial hall in Chapel Hill, a spectacular building that was destroyed. James Walker was chosen as contractor for the brick Georgian structure, which cost only $20,000 and came complete with stained-glass windows, a patterned slate roof, and a handsome spire. As in the subsequent building, construction also cost a life; George Wilson of Baltimore, the supervising brick mason, fell from the tower on July 6, 1860. The church was dedicated on April 28, 1861, 16 days after the Battle of Fort Sumter.

The steeple had a clock face in each of its four sides; all were maintained by the City of Wilmington and deemed, as a group, the "Town Clock." The spire also housed a large mellow-toned bell, a gift from George Harriss, which was rung to herald regular church services, weddings, funerals, and to broadcast a fire alarm. The sexton, who rang the bell among other duties, was a former slave who had accompanied his master onto Civil War battlefields. His winsome personality and exciting tales transfixed the boys of the congregation, who visited him often in his dirt-floored basement "office" that had been dug out just below the pulpit. Occasionally, the sexton sent the boys, including young Henry Bacon McKoy, into high glee by allowing them to climb the spire with him and ring the church bell. Mr. McKoy remembered the old building. "There was an ample balcony across the west end, reached by a wide stair just north of the main tower. I remember that (in the balcony) the deacons took collections by the means of a carpet covered box poked at you with a long stick."

Woodrow Wilson also spent time in the building; his father, Joseph R. Wilson, served as minister from November 1, 1874, until April 5, 1885, and returned to Wilmington again in 1899 for a year's stay. Though the future president was pursuing education and career during that time, he visited often enough to be remembered. "He rode a bicycle down Orange Street towards the river one day. He couldn't stop and went right in the water," recalled an eyewitness and fellow Presbyterian in 1978.

On New Year's Eve, 1925, shortly after a Sunday school meeting and party, smoke invaded the sanctuary. The church bell tolled mournfully one last time, summoning firemen who would be unable to tame the electrical fire already sending flames through the roof. John Hall, Martin Willard, B. Frank Hall, Thomas Hoke Hall, Henry MacMillan, Dr. A.D.P. Gilmour, Mary Hannis Whitted, and many others watched on that bitterly cold night as the main building, completely inflamed, burned brightly against a black sky. Helen Weathers McCarl remembered it over 50 years later as a "beautiful horror."

Those who saw the fire had one dramatic memory in common, forever emblazoned on their minds. Local artist Claude Howell, who watched the fire from the balcony of his home at the Carolina Apartments, expressed it succinctly. "I can see it clearly in my mind," he recounted in 1978. "The steeple became one giant flame and then fell with a great crash." Embers burned through the night, leading Thomas Hall to note, "The old church burned from 1925 into 1926."

The next morning, frozen water from the firemen's hoses had left ornate traceries and jagged icicles throughout the ruins. As for contents, comparatively little was salvaged, including a brass lectern, dragged out of the burning building by Martin Willard; a melted fragment of the church bell; Communion silver; and a baptismal bowl. Structurally, the old building did indeed have a firm foundation, which was reused in the south wall and a portion of the west wall of the 1928 Hobart Upjohn design that now graces the corner of Third and Orange Streets. The 1861 foundations, scattered brick and an apparently indestructible cornerstone from the 1818 church, which now rests on the tower floor, are all that remain of the first three First Presbyterian Church buildings. (1982.46.110.)

This photograph of the First Presbyterian Church Manse on the northwest corner of Fourth and Orange Streets was taken c. 1910 when Dr. John H. Wells was in residence. On the left is the rear of the 1861 red-brick church building. The manse was torn down in the 1960s. (Calder Collection.)

The cornerstone of Southside Baptist Church, located on the northwest corner of Fifth and Wooster Streets, was laid June 26, 1913. The church, designed by J.M. McMichael, served its communicants for almost 60 years, but vandalism prompted the congregation to move to South College Road in 1972. Some stained glass from the Fifth Street building was incorporated into the new church. (1991.40.2.)

The Sue McGinney Gregg House, pictured here in 1914, was located at 317 Princess Street. Built c. 1845 by the Odd Fellows, it served originally as the McGinney School. In 1936, it was razed and replaced by the Woodrow Wilson Hut, which had moved from Chesnut Street to make way for the new post office. The pump from the McGinney School still exists, in the park next to Thalian Hall. (1982.46.34.)

This image of the Formyduval School in Nakina was photographed c. 1900. The one-room Columbus County school typifies many such structures scattered throughout rural Cape Fear. (IA251.)

Cornelius Harnett School, located at 920 North Sixth Street, was initially a school for whites. In 1948, it became a black school known as Peabody Annex. In 1952, the school was renamed for James B. Dudley, a Wilmingtonian who served as president of the Agricultural and Technical College in Greensboro. (IA601.)

The East Wilmington School appeared this way in 1920, when East Wilmington simply meant Market Street, beyond Forest Hills. The building was subsidized in part by Julius Rosenwald, who established a $40 million trust in 1913 to improve and equip rural black schools. (University of North Carolina at Wilmington.)

Hemenway School, on Fourth Street between Red Cross and Campbell, was built in 1897. "The Hemenway School, Mr. James F. Post, architect and contractor, is as good as finished—all in two months," reported the *Morning Star* on August 22, 1897. The school, named for philanthropist Mary Hemenway, burned in 1913. (1980.1.8.)

In 1914, Burrett Stephens designed the second Hemenway School, located at 210 North Fifth Avenue. On May 16, 1971, after having been designated the board of education building, it also burned, taking with it the "permanent" records of thousands of former students. (North Carolina Collection, University of North Carolina Library at Chapel Hill.)

Williston Primary School, built in 1865 with funds from the American Missionary Association (AMA), was located on South Seventh Street between Ann and Nun Streets. In 1873, the AMA sold Williston to the New Hanover County Board of Education. The building was demolished in 1915. (University of North Carolina at Wilmington.)

Williston Normal School operated from 1866 to 1930. The building was named for Samuel Williston, a Massachusetts native who gave liberally to the American Missionary Society, the organization that built and funded the school. (University of North Carolina at Wilmington.)

This is Williston Industrial School, at 319 South Tenth Street, as it appeared c. 1930. This building burned in 1936. The Williston Alumni Association supports civic projects and funded the Williston Auditorium at Cape Fear Museum. (Louis T. Moore Collection, New Hanover County Public Library.)

The Gregory Community Center, located at 613 Nun Street, was built in 1881 by the American Missionary Association as a residence for teachers of the black community. Northerners, concerned with the educational needs of blacks, gave generously to the Gregory Community Center as well as to Gregory Congregational United Church of Christ, whose building still exists. (IA3119.)

In 1911–1912, Samuel Bear built Isaac Bear School as a memorial to his brother, who had died in 1911. The land, on Market Street between Twelfth and Thirteenth Streets, was purchased from Thomas H. Wright; architect J.F. Leitner drew the design. The University of North Carolina at Wilmington, known at the time as Wilmington College, began in this building in 1947. When the campus later moved to South College Road, university officials named one of the new buildings Bear Hall in honor of their first home. An auditorium, which had been added at the rear of the building, is all that remains of Isaac Bear School. (1979.12.1.)

In 1857, the U.S. Treasury Department purchased 50 acres of land in what was known as the "southeastern suburbs" as a site for a U.S. Marine Hospital. The plat extended to the boundaries of Eighth, Thirteenth, Ann, and Castle Streets, with the hospital placed on the corner of Eighth and Nun Streets. Architect Ammi B. Young designed the building; James Walker was the supervising contractor. Though the design was beautifully conceived, red tape took its toll.

"The Marine Hospital is a fine building, and an ornament to our town. But why is it not opened and put into operation? We understand that it has not yet been received by Government. How it is not why it is, is something that we cannot explain," reported the *Daily Herald*, March 6, 1860, months after it was completed. Though it opened eventually on a limited basis, in 1870, it was sold for $20,000, only to be repurchased by the government eight years later. Except for occasional National Guard meetings and occupancy by a group of WACS during World War II, the beautiful hospital was dormant from 1919 until its demolition in 1950. Plans drawn in the late 1940s by city architect James B. Lynch for a million-dollar civic auditorium on the site never came to fruition. (North Carolina Collection, University of North Carolina Library at Chapel Hill.)

Major funding for James Walker Memorial Hospital came from a stonemason, contractor, and builder who came to Wilmington in 1857 to supervise construction of the U.S. Marine Hospital. A native of Scotland, James Walker already had worked on the Capitol building and the Smithsonian before a temporary job location became his permanent home. After completing the U.S. Marine Hospital, he built the 1861 First Presbyterian Church, designed a residence for David R. Murchison at 305 South Third Street, served as supervising architect for the Temple of Israel and Tileston School, and spent ten years building the Institution for the Insane in Morganton.

Aware that he was in declining health, James Walker decided to bequeath a park to his adopted home, but was encouraged by Dr. W.J.H. Bellamy to give the city a public hospital instead. A site was chosen on the southeast corner of Ninth and Rankin Streets and the plans were drawn by Kenneth M. Murchison of New York. James Walker oversaw work on the hospital but died March 15, 1901, just before its completion. James Sprunt, the architect's brother-in-law, and William Gilchrist supervised the final stages of the project. Not only was the finished product functional, it was beautiful. Philadelphia pressed brick, 40 feet wide and 148 feet in length, was accented with brownstone trim. As one approached the entrance, graceful porches and an impressive porte cochere made it look more like a fine inn than a place where thousands of Wilmingtonians would take their first and last breaths. Inside, enameled beds, oak dressers, and washstands with basins and pitchers added comfort and familiarity. (1997.54.97.)

Initially, charity cases were admitted free with a permit from the county supervisor of health; paying patients could have a private room for as little as $17.50 a week. The main building housed rooms for white patients, administrative offices, a kitchen, and a laundry. Two other buildings were appended; William H. Sprunt donated one for the care of black patients and the housing of student nurses and the Samuel Bear family funded a building for the treatment of infectious diseases.

Space was added in 1905 specifically for the care of white women and children; black builder Valentine Howe Sr. completed most the work, but he, like James Walker, also died before the work was completed. The Marion Sprunt Wing was a gift to the city from Edward Payson George, James Sprunt, and Luola Murchison Sprunt in memory of the Sprunt's daughter. The little girl died in 1901, aged 13, after contracting scarlet fever at what her father labeled "a so-called health resort."

In 1914, after 13 years of operation, James Walker had admitted 1,407 patients, 767 white and 640 black, 772 pay cases and 635 charity patients. There were 19,409 days of treatment, and the average number of patients on any day was 53. It was noted that, "The institution can accommodate about eighty patients if they are properly apportioned as to color and sex." James Walker Hospital was demolished in 1972. (1997.054.0097.)

Harper Sanitarium, on the northeast corner of Front and Castle Streets, was founded by Dr. Charles T. Harper and was built for $7,500. The first floor was divided into two storefronts, one of which was a drugstore. The second floor contained 12 rooms, one of which was used for surgery. Later, the building housed Southside Pharmacy. (IA352.)

This was the Niestlies Drug Store at 415 North Seventh Street as it looked c. 1900. William Niestle, a white pharmacist, manufactured drugs and sold them from his house. In 1920, Dr. Foster Burnett, a black physician, bought the building and transformed it into the first Community Hospital. In 1938, the hospital moved to new facilities and this building later was razed. The dental office of Dr. Suzette Gause and Dr. Roger Gause has now replaced it. (1984.88.3.)

Community Hospital reopened in 1939, in a gleaming new building designed by James B. Lynch. W.L. Jewell, a contractor from Sanford, built the $49,700 structure. Here, the building serves as background for a Gregory School ceremony, c. 1960. (1983.34.31.)

The YMCA building at 301–305 North Front Street was built in 1891. It contained a large auditorium that was used for many purposes including concerts and religious revival services. After 1912, the building became the O'Berry and, later, Brunswick Hotel. (IA695.)

Work began on the "new" YMCA on December 10, 1912; on October 1, 1913, the organization moved from its smaller headquarters at Front and Grace Streets to the building pictured here. D.H. Penton was president and J.B. Huntington served as general secretary. Boys' basketball games drew large crowds, and swimming lessons went on year-round. Rooms were usually rented by the month, but a few were rented by the day to seamen in port. The building was destroyed July 20, 1970. (1992.78.37.)

"Our friend, Capt. W.R. Kenan, has been edifying us with some of his jokes this morning. Of course, he spoke a few lines about [fire] insurance and wound up by asking us, 'Why is Ann Street the last street in Wilmington?' We gave it up and he answered, 'Because Nun was beyond it.' "

The Boys' Brigade met in the basement of Immanuel Presbyterian Church on South Front Street from 1896 until this new armory was dedicated on June 22, 1905. The four-story Norman structure on the southeast corner of Second and Church Streets was a gift from Mary Lily Kenan Flagler, a modest outlay from the same family purse that would fund schools, auditoriums, and Kenan Stadium. However, the Boys' Brigade Armory was more personal to Mrs. Henry Flagler, who grew up in Wilmington and was a friend of Colonel Walker Taylor, founder of the local club. Mary Lily's father, William Rand Kenan, was a sponsor of the Boy's Brigade Armory and had accompanied Colonel Taylor on many outings, including camping trips to Southport. Mr. Kenan died in 1903; Mary Lily gave the building as a memorial to him.

Charles McMillen was architect and R.H. Brady, contractor, of what one critic described as "grim grandeur." The exterior was composed of "patent stone," hollow concrete that appeared solid. At the same time the Brigade was under construction, Mr. Brady was building an investment property of his own at 610 South Third Street. He used the same patent stone material on the house that can be seen today as an example of the exterior finish of the Boy's Brigade Armory.

Inside, boys who maintained a good attendance record in any Sunday school could enjoy the bowling alley, dining room, auditorium, and a gymnasium so compact that the wall and the basketball boundary line were the same. The handsome library, filled with 2,000 leather-bound books donated by James Sprunt, prompted one reporter to write that it seemed the sort of place "where Dukes and Earls and the like were wont to sit and smoke and delve into the secrets of voluminous books." For some, the elegance of the library was eclipsed by another thing they did not have at home "an up-to-date shower bath apartment . . . with hot water rushing through the pipes."

Governor R.B. Glenn dedicated the new building in a well-planned ceremony that proved as unpredictable as the general behavior of young boys. When Governor Glenn was delivering his speech, a photographer's flash exploded, "the report of which approached the volume of a cannon." Someone in an unguarded moment yelled, "Fire," and the audience began stampeding from the hall. Twelve women fainted and the governor himself sank back into his chair, exclaiming, "Oh, God."

Colonel Taylor and Captain James Metts tried to calm the crowd and a quartet and pianist broke into a droning melody in an attempt to thwart the panic. One brave man blocked the new circular staircase to prevent further stampeding; however, "he soon found that more active persons were jumping over his head and flying to the street." The newspaper account concluded, "The affair was quite the most exciting of its kind ever witnessed in Wilmington and the memory of it will long remain with those who experienced it."

The armory bustled with activity for the next 45 years as underprivileged boys played hard, attended lectures, banquets, dramas, and concerts. In 1950, the Boys' Brigade Armory moved to a new home at 718 South Third Street and the building was sold. The Brigade building *had* been a gift from Mary Lily Kenan Flagler and the boys did indeed bear arms during drill practice. However, in its last years, the building functioned as a tenement house and its misspelled name, "Lilly Arms," was ambiguous. The building was razed *c.* 1960. (IA1521.)

"To a very large number of human beings, the cemetery is a place of resort; imparting sensations of interest, that, however melancholy, are satisfying," wrote one Wilmingtonian in 1889 of Oakdale. Indeed, Wilmington's oldest and largest cemetery has been the haunt of the living since 1855.

In 1869, 14 years after the first body was interred at Oakdale Cemetery, the board of directors noted a need "to have a rustic lodge, to be located on the grounds." Not only would the lodge contain a bell, "to lend additional solemnity to sad occasions," but it would give mourners, especially females, a sheltered seat upon which to escape rain, scorching sun, fatigue, and grief-induced vertigo. It was not to be a rush job. By the spring of 1871, a two-room open shelter fitted with benches and a tiny belfry sat near the old Miller Street entrance to Oakdale. Two years later, the doors and windows arrived by steamer from New York.

The directors and lot owners were justifiably proud of the charming lodge when finally complete and curiously boastful of Oakdale's increased occupancy. Often, burial figures for the year were published in the local paper, complete with causes of death listed by category. Limited by 19th-century diagnostic tools, final blows were attributed to everything from "supposed suicide" to "teething." As gravesites filled, visitors increased and soon the "City of the Dead" bustled with life, especially on weekends. Hitching posts were installed and Oakdale's new "streets" were made plenty wide for a horse and carriage. Policemen were requested to monitor the crowds, catch flower thieves, and reprimand children who tried to chase the cemetery rabbits, who had grown populous by nature and tame by treats from picnicking visitors.

The lodge remained a focal point of Oakdale activity, but only lasted 25 years. Early in the morning of February 20, 1896, three workmen gathered in the lodge and built a fire in the stove. A few minutes later, a defective flue sent sparks raining down on them. They immediately went to work to squelch the fire and issue an alarm, but before firemen arrived, the building and the magnolia tree next to it burned to the ground. Early Oakdale records and plans survived, thanks to the cemetery employees' presence of mind. The building is pictured here, *c.* 1890. (New Hanover County Public Library.)

Four days after the first Oakdale Cemetery Lodge burned, Oakdale officials decided to rebuild on the same site. James F. Post designed the $5,000 building and H.A. Tucker served as contractor. Built on a granite foundation, the new lodge was made of North Carolina brownstone and was roofed in slate. Buffed stone was used to trim the corners, doors, and windows; copper was used for the finials. The 40-foot tower housed a bell and the superintendent's office. A tiled entrance led to the main room, measuring 34 feet by 24 feet, which was designed to host both sacred and secular meetings. A large bay window on the south end doubled as a casket door for funerals. An additional stained-glass window memorialized the cemetery's founders Armand J. deRosset, Edward Kidder, Platt K. Dickinson, William A. Wright, Oscar G. Parsley, Dugald McMillan, John A. Taylor, John L. Meares, Charles D. Ellis, Henry Nutt, Stephen D. Wallace, John MacRae, James Cassidey, Stephen B. Polly, and George R. French.

James Post was praised heartily for his design. "If no monument is ever reared to his memory the beautiful brownstone lodge at Oakdale cemetery, designed and built under his supervision, will be a lasting testimonial of his useful career," stated the *Messenger*, July 16, 1899. Unfortunately, positioning of the lodge had not been farsighted. Drainage problems always had dogged the Miller Street entrance and, in 1915, the present entrance at the north end of Fifteenth Street was established. Architectural accolades aside, the lodge soon was deemed a financial drain and destroyed. Some of the stone now lines the Willetts family plot. Granite columns, also designed by James F. Post, have been moved from the old entrance and now stand at the Live Oak section of the cemetery. (IA1678.)

Ruth Hall, located at 401 South Seventh Street, was built in 1888 as headquarters for the Wilmington Grand United Order of Odd Fellows, a black organization. The three-story brick structure featured a large concert hall where noted musicians performed and where lectures were delivered on everything from the fine arts to patriotism. Ruth Hall was torn down in the 1940s. (1980.1.8.)

The design of the 1922 Cape Fear Country Club building is attributable to Leslie N. Boney, partner of architect James F. Gause. Though the building, photographed in 1996 by Freda Wilkins, still stands, it will be replaced soon by a larger facility. When this one opened, club officials reported that it had "all the modern conveniences such as heat, water and electricity." The surrounding golf course contains Confederate earthworks and two small family cemeteries.

Three

THE MARKETPLACE

It's amazing what a railroad, an ocean, and a river can do for industry. Everyone from enterprising newcomers to conservative locals capitalized on the convenience of the port and the ease of transporting goods inland. Large wholesale businesses abounded, but pluck and horse sense brought prosperity to small merchants as well. As fortunes increased, a wealth of buildings emerged.

In 1945, this was the scene looking north on Front Street from Chestnut. J.C. Penney and Western Union mingled with locally owned businesses like Saffo's Restaurant, Peoples Furniture, and The Julia, as the Elks Building mascot looked on. (1985.72.46.)

"Wilmington is chiefly composed of two streets crossing each other, the one running parallel to the River. The market place stands in the place where the two streets meet; this was a capital error as it interrupts the prospect every way," wrote glib traveler William Mylne in the 1770s. In 1848, locals, unmoved by his words, built a new market house, deemed a "beautiful superstructure," on virtually the same spot as the old bright yellow one. The location was the residential and commercial heart of Wilmington for more than a century. Many prominent citizens resided there, like Governor William Tryon, who, before moving the state capitol to New Bern, had a townhouse on the south side of the street.

The scene was enhanced by as many as 100 ships docking in the Cape Fear River every day, making it a sort of world bazaar within the provincial city. As if horses, carriages, carts, and pedestrians did not create enough activity to watch from the iron balconies that used to line the block, canoes occasionally paddled past toward the intersection of Second and Market Streets, where the "Mud Market" thrived. The Mud Market was a separate site usually reserved for the smelly business of selling seafood in a time when ice was a luxury. Before a system of subterranean tunnels harnessed the brook, Jacob's Run, the lower end of the street, was navigable only to small flat-bottomed boats.

Contractor Benjamin Gardner, a former resident of Savannah, supervised the work on the 1848 market house, which extended down Market Street from Front Street toward the Cape Fear River. The stylized colonnade measured 187 by 25 feet. Thirty-eight cast-iron columns supported a plaster ceiling, iron roof, and a tower that housed a 565-pound bell. Influenced by John Norris's work in Savannah, Mr. Gardner probably also designed the stylized structure, complete with a neoclassical crest above the belfry. His artistry was applauded by the local newspaper as follows: "The height of the stalls and the lightness of the racks offers little obstruction to the view across the street and leaves the architectural proportion and beauty of the columns undiminished."

Ten vendors' stalls, each delegated either to fish, meat, or vegetables, filled the brick-floored market. The bell, procured in 1751 to replace drums as the usual municipal routing call, was the main feature on the second floor of the market house. James Sprunt wrote that it "was rung at nine o'clock, one o'clock and seven o'clock; and it rang the nine o'clock curfew, which required all slaves without a pass to leave the street." On special occasions, bells were not enough. Black trumpeter Philip Bassadier played reveille at the market to note holidays and military events.

The west end of the market afforded a good view of the ancient ducking stool, a seat attached to a large wooden beam that could be lowered into the Cape Fear to punish and embarrass local lawbreakers. Another unusual sight was the Christmas Kooners, blacks in fancy costumes who sang and danced for large crowds around town. On New Year's Eve, they rode horseback through the streets to the market house, where they staged a mock wedding of Old Testament figures Rebecca and Isaac. Year round, nomadic performers plied their trade around the market.

In a controversial move, the market house was torn down January 20, 1881, after the City moved meat vending to the market on Front Street between Dock and Orange. Alfred Howe, a talented black builder who had purchased the old building from the City of Wilmington for $150, razed it throughout the rainy day, noting that "every timber was still sound." The tower fell at four in the afternoon, but the ancient bell had already been removed and was installed later in the fire station at Fourth and Campbell Streets. Maybe Alfred Howe "recycled" all that sound timber, possibly incorporating it into the McKoy House, a James Post design that Howe built at 402 South Third Street.

The "Paradise Tree," probably named for the scarcity of shade, can be glimpsed on the far left side of the photograph. The tree and a telegraph pole nearby were cut down seven days after the market was razed. Despite the fact that everything was leveled and the rubble had been removed, loyalties to the old market house ran deep for weeks. Several vendors refused to trade at the new market, including one salty proprietor of a fish cart. When instructed to move from what had become merely the street, he cried that he " 'Wouldn't by a damned sight.' Then he wheeled his horse about and started in the direction from whence he came." (1976.55.56.)

This photograph of a naval store yard, stocked with tar and resin, was taken c. 1895 from the west side of the Governor Dudley Mansion. From the vantage point of a stairway that no longer exists, the railway is visible across James Sprunt's land. He gated the Nun Street side, but furnished a key to the railroad conductor. (1984.70.192.)

Saturating wood with creosote made good timber stronger and inferior types of lumber marketable. In 1886, inventors Louis A. Hanson and Andrew Smith came to Wilmington to establish the Carolina Oil and Creosote Company on the Cape Fear River. This photograph of a local creosote plant and an unidentified man was taken c. 1920. (1981.1.100.)

The Worth and Worth wharf, pictured here c. 1880, was located on the river side of Water Street between Grace and Walnut Streets. They shared the wharf with Alexander Sprunt and Sons. As agents of the Cape Fear Steamboat Company, Worth and Worth built the *A.P. Hurt*, *Flora McDonald*, and *Governor Worth*. (1979.11.11.)

This photograph of Worth and Worth was taken c. 1890 when local businessmen Jonathan and David Gaston Worth had a thriving business marketing wholesale groceries, lime, and cement. The building was later occupied by the Independent Ice Company. (1984.70.18.)

This detail from an animated 1932 Claude Howell drawing shows Water Street, looking south from Chestnut Street. Narrow old cars fit nicely on the train tracks and women still used their heads to carry vegetables back and forth to the present-day City Market.

C.D. Maffitt's Supply House (located where the Wachovia parking lot now stands) was established as a ships' chandlery in 1885. In 1912, the firm moved into this building, designed by Henry Emil Bonitz and built by R.H. Brady, on the northeast corner of Princess and Water Streets. Like many of Mr. Bonitz's buildings, it featured Borden brick, manufactured by the Borden family in Goldsboro, the architect's hometown.

Clarence Dudley Maffitt, colorful founder of the supply house, described himself as one "who reformed from a globe circling seafaring career to settle down and make good." His nautical interests and a gift for expression came honestly. He was the son of legendary sea captain John Newland Maffitt by his third wife, author Emma Hamblin Maffitt. (Private collection.)

Only a few years later, this was the scene on Water Street, looking north from Princess Street. The corner and balconies of the Maffitt building are visible on the far right. As downtown's waterway emptied, so did these shipping offices. A park and the Coast Guard dock now occupy this site. (1994.4.111.)

This photograph was taken April 4, 1957, by Henry B. McKoy, who labeled it, "The last iron balcony left." Iron balconies, both ornamental and functional, once graced most downtown buildings. A Neuwirth Brothers truck sits close to the ornamented Flowers Metal Works building at 15 North Second Street. Both the balcony and the building are now gone. (1984.70.127.)

Alexander Sprunt and Son, once the single largest cotton brokerage firm in the country, occupied this building at Nutt and Walnut Streets. Farmers and merchants brought bales of cotton to loading docks, located along a wharf 1,000 feet long. Inside, a massive machine, appropriately called a "compress," squeezed each bale to half its size to save storage and shipping costs. The machinery broke down only once for any significant time. In 1876, though inactive for only a few hours, the shutdown created a traffic jam on the river, with 26 vessels at the mercy of a mechanic. Sprunt's first Champion Compress and 1,500 bales of cotton were destroyed by fire on October 3, 1879. The building pictured was built c. 1887 and was large enough to store 10,000 bales of cotton. It was used later as a sugar warehouse.

In addition to being a successful businessman, owner James Sprunt was a local historian, a philanthropist, and a deeply religious man who supported medical missions overseas and helped build several Wilmington churches, for both white and black congregations. As he was more than just a businessman, this building became more than just a warehouse.

On March 18, 1888, the first large evangelistic meetings in Wilmington convened here and were held until April 11. The hall was fitted with benches, and thousands of people attended every service. In 1893, world-renowned evangelist Dwight L. Moody came to Wilmington and conducted services at Alexander Sprunt and Son for three weeks, beginning on March 18, 1893. The meeting, "held in the large compartment of the Champion Compress," was integrated and Mr. Moody was said to be "greatly interested in the singing of the colored people who occupied a corner of the large auditorium." (IA3983.)

The general office building of Alexander Sprunt and Son was designed by Henry Bonitz and built on the northeast corner of Front and Walnut Streets, a site laid vacant when the Front Street Methodist Church burned February 21, 1886. Within months, construction began on this brick building, which was trimmed in granite. Later, the building pictured was utilized as the Shamrock Cafe and the Parker Seed Company. (Duke University, Special Collections Library.)

In 1920, the Alexander Sprunt and Son office was relocated to a new structure at 321 North Front Street; this Henry Bonitz design still stands. This interior shot, taken in January 1922, represents another scene that won't be replicated; there were no cubicles, no fluorescent lights, and no particleboard. (Duke University, Special Collections Library.)

Tradition states that the Bank of Cape Fear building at 17 North Front Street was once the home of merchant John Ancrum. He owned several ships, died in 1779, and lies securely entombed, having been buried in the portion of St. James Cemetery that is now under Market Street. In 1806, seven years after John Ancrum's death, Joshua G. Wright, president of the bank, purchased this property for $3,400.

The Bank of Cape Fear thrived and soon had offices in seven other cities. The bank building had a major setback on January 17, 1840, when a fire of mysterious origin broke out at John Dawson's store on the northeast corner of Front and Market Streets. With the exception of two buildings, everything was destroyed from Second Street to the river in the first block of North Front Street. Though not destroyed, the Bank of Cape Fear was badly damaged. Architect John S. Norris happened to be in town to build Thomas U. Walter's design for St. James Church. The Bank of Cape Fear directors, many of whom were on the church vestry, asked Norris to also repair the bank building. The result was a facade that recalls many of Norris's designs in Savannah.

Captain John H.K. Burgwin, the grandson of John Burgwin, a former director, died in 1847. Joshua G. Wright Jr. delivered a eulogy to Captain Burgwin, a Mexican War hero, from the portico of the Bank of Cape Fear. A monument, later moved to Oakdale Cemetery, was erected to Captain Burgwin in the small park behind the bank.

After the Civil War, the Bank of Cape Fear dissolved. In 1868, John Dawson's brother James purchased the building for $105,000 and operated the Banking House of James Dawson from the main floor. He removed the beautiful staircase and set up a stagecoach company in the basement. In 1878, James Dawson merged his bank with the First National Bank. The building was razed in 1899, to make room for the Masonic Temple, which still stands.

Three prominent Wilmingtonians who served as officials in the bank resided in the building during their employment; these men included Col. James Burr, Henry Russell Savage, and Isaac Bates Grainger. (1982.3.4.)

The Bank of New Hanover was incorporated in 1872; by April 1873, it was already bullish enough to have constructed an elegant home on the northwest corner of Front and Princess Streets. Architect Samuel Sloan, contractor Joseph McIllwaine, and the foreman John Wright, all residents of Philadelphia, supervised the rapid construction of the four-story building. The $40,000 building was constructed of brick with a massive stuccoed iron facade, slate mansard roof, and a full basement. The fourth floor was an assembly hall measuring 49 by 29 feet. All materials were brought from Philadelphia with the exception of the brick and Carolina yellow pine.

After 1902, a series of different banks occupied the building, including the Atlantic National Bank of Wilmington, the National Bank of Wilmington, and the People's Bank. Like the Orton Hotel during the 1920s and '30s, there was a barbershop in the basement where an extra quarter would buy you a hot shower. The structure was demolished in 1959 to make way for the Wachovia Bank building, a controversial move fought by mansard-roof aficionados, but cited by others as an example of how Wilmington had, "pulled itself up from antiquity and stagnation." (1976.55.58.)

The Southern Building, owned by Matt Heyer and designed by Charles McMillen, sat on the southwest corner of Front and Chestnut Streets. It housed an array of offices. Attorney John D. Bellamy, the Episcopal Diocese of North Carolina, architect Burrett Stephens, Hugh MacRae, Julian K. Taylor, and cotton broker Harry G. Latimer all leased space here at one time or another. (1981.26.2.)

Martin Stevenson Willard, owner of Carolina Insurance Company, was a North Carolina legislator and veteran chairman of the New Hanover County Commissioners. His Tuscan-style house, located on the southeast corner of Sixth and Orange Streets, still stands. This photograph of his office building at 10 Princess Street was taken in 1916, as workmen readied the site for the present U.S. Custom House. (IA4867.)

"Mr. J.H. Rehder has returned from New York, where he purchased a large stock of holiday goods for his mammoth department store at Fourth Street Bridge," reported the *Morning Star* on November 15, 1899. The J.H. Rehder Company was established in 1887 and thrived until the Great Depression. Located at 617 North Fourth Street, it supplied customers with everything from fancy hats to carpets. This photograph was taken in 1902, which was about the time John Rehder began a highly successful mail order program. (IA1546.)

The northeast corner of Front and Market Streets was the business address of merchant John Dawson until January 1840, when it and many other buildings burned in the famous "Dawson Fire." It was replaced by this building. After Dawson died in 1881, druggists J.K. McIlhenny and, later, William H. Green and Company occupied this cozy corner building at the intersection of Front and Market Streets. However, in 1910, it was razed to make room for the hiccup of Wilmington's skyline—the Atlantic Trust and Banking Company Building. (1980.21.11.)

"Shrewsburys on Shell, Green Sea Turtle, Quenelles, and Gelee au Vin de Champagne," read the Thanksgiving menu at the Orton Hotel, November 24, 1892. Visitors such as Thomas Edison, who visited Wilmington in 1899, enjoyed the elegant dining room where the white linens were spotless and waiters stood tall in full dress. However, the Orton had not always been so fancy. An earlier hotel had sat closer to Water Street on the same lot and was incorporated into the new plan at 109–117 North Front Street by the owner, Colonel K.M. Murchison. "A connection between the old and new Orton has been made by an arch cut through the walls of the buildings," the local newspaper announced in 1887.

Colonel Murchison, who also owned Orton Plantation, employed architect J.A. Wood, contractor J.S. Allen, and superintendent James Walker to erect a solid brick 100-room hotel that would be Wilmington's most elegant inn for the next 40 years. A two-story gingerbread verandah was the hallmark of the Orton. It ran the entire length of the building and had an elliptical indentation at the center that enabled a guest on the second floor to have a view of the first floor. "Rare and beautiful flowers" filled conservatories on both sides.

In addition to the main doors, gentlemen had the option of their own entrance, to the left; the ladies entrance was to the right. Once inside, everyone was feted to a lavish interior. German beveled mirrors, carved cherry mantels, crystal chandeliers, and heavy imported rugs created a rich environment for visitors from afar and a "home away from home" for many privileged Wilmingtonians. The final stage of refurbishment, in 1888, provided for steam heat, electric lights, and "a hydraulic elevator of the latest pattern, with an elegant upholstered car with mirrors in the panels."

Hotel Wilmington, Wilmington, N. C.

In the 1920s, the Hotel Cape Fear and the Hotel Wilmington opened. With newer, bigger options, business soon waned at the Orton, which was then owned by Aaron Abrams. On January 21, 1949, the old inn caught fire; 40 guests were in the house. Despite a number of stairways that had been touted as "easy and rapid exits in case of fire," the quick acceleration of the flames caused a number of guests to jump from the second-floor veranda. The story of the spectacular fire and the million-dollar loss was carried in newspapers as far away as Boston. Today, Bessie's, the basement space that was once an opulent billiard parlor, is the only thing left of Wilmington's grandest hotel. It was still operating as a poolroom in 1953, when Willie Mosconi sank 365 balls in a row to set the world pocket billiards record. (1980.21.9.)

The Stuart House in Southport was a distinguished little inn where conversation was the primary entertainment. Mary E. Stuart, a widow from Tennessee, bought the house and converted it into an inn in 1842. Her daughter Kate took over after her mother's death and became a local legend. In 1917, Colonel Fred Olds interviewed Kate Stuart, the legendary Southport innkeeper. "Nothing could be more delightful than to sit in the charming old parlor at Miss Kate's after tea and hear her tell stories. Known to thousands of North Carolinians, she is a delightful link between the old days before the Civil War and this present time. She can remember when the soldiers who had gone from North Carolina to Mexico came home again in 1848." She also regaled her guests with tales of the Civil War, when Southport was the only place in the Confederacy where gold pieces circulated and where pilots got $5,000 for making a run out from Nassau.

Because Southport was Brunswick's county seat, her guest list was heavy on attorneys. However, the clientele was not limited by profession. Civil engineer Henry Bacon moved his whole family into Miss Kate's for a short stay in 1876. Wilmington businessmen, young couples, and old friends often traveled to Miss Kate's on the steamer *Wilmington*.

The house would accommodate 40 guests, but some rooms were obviously more desirable than others. James Sprunt wrote to Kate Stuart in 1906, "My cousin, Valeria Sprunt, has just passed through a severe attack of illness and is now convalescing in Dillon, S.C. She needs a change . . . and will accept my proposal to be my guest to your house at Southport. I write to ask if you will kindly provide for her the best you have in the way of a room upstairs—not the middle back room, however."

The Stuart House was destroyed during Hurricane Hazel in 1954. Photographer George Nevens snapped this picture *c.* 1938. (1988.39.56.)

The Colonial Inn, owned by Oscar Pearsall, occupied one of the best corners in town: the northeast corner of Third and Market Streets. Mr. Pearsall and his brother Philander Pearsall were wholesale grocers with partner Benjamin Franklin Hall. Oscar Pearsall had already made real estate news in 1894, when he transported his Carolina Beach cottage "through the sounds on floats, to Wrightsville," where it was rebuilt.

In the spring of 1903, Oscar Pearsall moved a two-story frame residence, yet another A.J. deRosset House, and replaced it in 1903 with the apartment building pictured here in this c. 1920 photograph. It included a beautiful dining room where ladies wearing white gloves enjoyed afternoon tea.

In 1913, Mr. Pearsall took on another building project, but this time it was a church, Pearsall Memorial Presbyterian. Coincidentally, the church's most famous minister, Dr. B. Frank Hall, was a grandson of the Pearsalls' old business partner. The Colonial Inn burned on April 25, 1962. (IA380.)

J.H. "Foxy" Howard and Percy Wells formed a partnership in 1906 to start the first motion picture theater in the state. After a successful three-night stint at the Academy of Music, known today as Thalian Hall, they moved their business to 211 North Front Street, where they set up a 200-foot-long carnival tent, capable of seating 500. One huge bulb, hanging loosely from the center pole, lit the little palace between shows. Sawdust was spread liberally for a floor, and a respectable two-story wooden arch was erected as an entrance.

Percy Wells soon became a familiar sight, standing out in front of the theater, crying, "Come on in, folks. We're never over. We're never out. New picture showing! For five cents, the twentieth part of a dollar." Mr. Wells, a.k.a. the Great Percino, was a former trapeze artist with the Barnum and Bailey Circus and had been working solo in Wilmington from 1904 until 1906, performing on Market Street between Water and Front Streets. His partner, Foxy Howard, had once owned a carnival where he had met Percy Wells years earlier in Chicago. At the Bijou, Mr. Howard usually worked inside the tent, often coaxing customers who had spent a whole day watching the same movie to relinquish their seats. Caesar, Mr. Howard's Great Dane, wandered in and out at will; rats frequently scavenged the floor for peanuts. Like today, snacks were not in proportion to the price of admission. One nickel would buy you a seat and another one would purchase a treat from the "peanuts and popcorn boy," whose entrance was always heralded by a streak of white light across the screen. The only air conditioning provided included the raising of all the tent flaps between shows. In winter, heat came from a pot-bellied stove too hot to be near and too unradiant to be effective at a distance.

Some of the earliest movies shown at the Bijou included *The Great Train Robbery*, *Golden Hair and the Three Bears*, and *The Whole Damn Family and the Little Damn Dog*. Documentaries like *Scenes and Customs of India* were fascinating to theatergoers who seldom traveled and could not even envisage a television set. Sometimes flesh and blood celebrities would appear at the Bijou. In 1918, Emmet Dalton, an aged former member of the "Dalton Gang," appeared to discuss the mistakes of his youth. Another show, *Mutt and Jeff*, featured, "pretty girls, sparkling music, and scintillating and elaborate scenic effect."

Tent seating consisted of benches, which were later replaced by folding wooden chairs tied together in rows. The left-hand corner of the tent was roped off for blacks. Sometimes as a film was being rewound by hand, everyone joined in for sing-a-longs as words were flashed on the screen. Mrs. Percy Wells, Mildred Kornegay, and Frank Bancks played the piano during the silent movies: "Hearts and Flowers" for the romantic scenes and "The William Tell Overture" for suspense. During intermission, Mrs. Wells played and sang favorites like "Pony Boy." It was a far cry from Mrs. Wells's earlier days when, using the stage name "Alice Fisher," she sang to Broadway audiences and hobnobbed with friends like Lionel Barrymore, Florence Ziegfeld, and Lillian Russell.

In 1910, Foxy Howard and Percy Wells purchased the land they had been leasing from J.W. Murchison and W.E. Perdew and began work with architect Burrett H. Stephens to plan a permanent theater. The following year, a heavy snow destroyed the canvas just as they were about to complete the new building. Contractor R.H. Brady usually built much less glitzy structures, like the MacRae Iron Front Building at 25 North Front Street, including the 1919 Tileston wing and the Fire Engine House at 602 North Fourth Street. Mirrored doors, a towering facade adorned with plaster figures, and gleaming tile floors set the Bijou apart from nearby buildings. Percy Wells continued to hawk the place, often in a voice that could be heard several blocks away. Foxy Howard, whose nickname came from "Foxy Grandpa," a cartoon character who, like Mr. Howard, was large and had a shock of white hair, had lost his Great Dane, but a Dalmatian now roamed the new theater.

Sometimes a 12-piece orchestra drowned out the tones of the small pipe organ, but fresh roses and an electric fan never quite obliterated the "atmosphere of the workaday folks." The Bijou, still the only show in town, continued to attract anybody and everybody. One writer for the *Morning Star* reported that the crowd was so diverse, you might even see a "debutante in luxurious furs accompanied by the town's butter and egg man."

After the new Bijou was judged a success, the owners began building a sequence of five more theaters and, in 1925, purchased Greenfield Lake. They hired Carl Rehder to handle public relations for their growing business. It was Mr. Rehder, in the depths of the Great Depression, who staged the "Collard Movie Show" at the Bijou. Admission was a head of collards; the "proceeds" were collected by the American Red Cross and sold to help fund their organization.

Jacob M. Sulke purchased the Bijou in 1933, but the theater already had seen its best years. It closed in 1956. All that remains of it now is a small park and a patch of the 1912 tile floor that reads "Bijou." (IA746.)

With the Bijou a runaway success, owners Foxy Howard and Percy Wells contracted architect Burrett H. Stephens to design another theater, the Royal. This one was built at 151 North Front Street on the site of the "old Air Dome," an open-air vaudeville and motion-picture theater established in 1911. This is how the Royal looked on October 29, 1945, when Henry Sternberger snapped this photograph from the post office steps. (1985.72.57.)

In July 1936, post office construction laid Post Office Alley bare. The three-story brick building, used primarily as a tenement, housed the Wilmington Art Gallery in the late 1950s. The organization later merged with St. John's Art Gallery. (U.S. Postal Service.)

In the 1940s, the old Gieschen Brothers Atlantic Inn and Cafe building, on the southeast corner of Front and Red Cross Streets, operated as headquarters for government projects. It housed everything from a Camp Davis school to canning and gardening classes. After passenger service ceased across the street at Union Station, the building was razed. (1980.53.171.)

"Wanted Large quantity of dewberries or blackberries, for wine making. Sol. Bear and Co.," read the ads in 1906, beckoning locals to the Sol. Bear and Company Winery at 702 North Front Street. In 1927, after the Bear family leased the building to Block's Cantfade Shirts and the Nehi Bottling Company, a fire destroyed part of the four-story building. This photograph, taken in the 1930s, depicts the new facade and Sigmond Bear's car. (IA4782.)

Workmen inspected and weighed cotton at Alexander Sprunt and Son's Champion Compress as sailing ships waited at the wharf. This photograph was taken c. 1885. (1980.1.8.)

During the 1930s, the Emergency Relief Administration operated a mattress factory in Levi McKoy Moseley's building at 615 Nixon Street. Sixteen women, including Mr. Moseley's daughter Margaret Williams, assembled mattresses for the needy. Levi Moseley's sister, Augusta Moseley Cooper, was a noted Wilmington leader and historic preservationist. (IA2988.)

"Great Fires" were local conflagrations vile enough to level a city block. After each fire, the smoldering ruins would be labeled the "burnt district, . . . full of unseemly masses of brick and rubbish." Then, like pruning's aftermath, a flurry of new buildings would occur; 247 new buildings were constructed in 1883 alone. Despite the fact that great hunks of the city burned repeatedly, firemen were revered by the general public, as they should have been for their efforts and bravery. However, insurance agents, owners of burning homes, and sometimes the press were quick to criticize.

"When we arrived, the entire building was wrapped in flames and hissing streams of water were feebly disputing the passage of the dread element," wrote an *Evening Post* reporter in 1873, echoing many such reports.

This blaze, though not labeled a "great fire," was pretty important to Samuel Bear, whose building at 18 Market Street was gutted on October 17, 1908.

In the Wilmington of 1899, $250,000 could buy you a brand new textile mill and a subdivision on 100 acres of land. That sum is what stockholders paid to purchase the land, which was once a camp for Confederate soldiers from W.A. Wright, and construct a building so immense it took 3 million bricks to contain it. Located on the site of an artesian well referred to as "Mineral Springs," the mill building dominated the western end of Shell Road (Wrightsville Avenue); employees' residences nearby created a village that thrived for six decades within the city.

Delgado Mills was owned principally by Edwin C. Holt of Burlington; it was named in honor of his wife, Dolores Delgado Stevens. Though Mr. Holt was the chief stockholder and original president of Delgado Cotton Mills, today his name is more closely associated with the house he and his wife built in Carolina Heights: the Holt-Wise Mansion at 1713 Market Street. Now utilized as the University of North Carolina at Wilmington for the Alumni Affairs office, the structure was built in 1907 and sold to Jessie Kenan Wise in 1916.

Delgado's original directors included Mr. Holt, Colonel K.M. Murchison, General Julian S. Carr, James H. Chadbourn, and R.R. Bellamy. The contractors, H.C. Zackary and A.D. Zackary, also built the North Carolina Insane Asylum in Raleigh and the Carolina Inn in Chapel Hill. The Delgado plans called for 6-inch-thick wood floors, a 125-foot chimney, and the installation of 10,000 spindles and 500 looms. (1992.31.505.)

Architect Charles McMillen designed the Odd Fellows Building on the northwest corner of Third and Princess Streets in 1904. The offices were occupied primarily by attorneys, including Addison Hewlett Jr., Marsden Bellamy, Aaron Goldberg, and Wallace Murchison. Waccamaw Bank bought the property and tore the building down in 1967, not long after this photograph was taken. Originally, a third-floor passageway on the north side of this building connected it to a medical school (not shown) next door. The College of Physicians and Surgeons was built in 1871, when medical degrees came more easily, specialists were few, and a prognoses could seem like a coin toss. "Mr. Kidder's condition is about the same," wrote James Sprunt in 1906. "He has recently spent several weeks at the Hot Springs where the doctor told him his case has been greatly exaggerated. On the other hand Mr. Flagler's physician in Florida, who sent him to the Hot Springs, told him he might die at any moment." (1992.78.52.)

The streetcar stop at the intersection of Park Avenue and Live Oak Parkway was a beauty, designed by James B. Lynch and Henry Bonitz. Now, according to architectural historian Edward F. Turberg, "only the concrete posts bordering the parking area survive." This photograph was taken in 1920. (1987.23.5.)

This photograph of the Thomas Quinlivan Horse Shoeing Forge at Third and Princess Streets was taken c. 1905. Mr. Quinlivan and his brother Daniel immigrated to the United States after Daniel was tried in his native Ireland for forging weapons with which to fight the Crown. The judge waived execution and the Quinlivans arrived in Wilmington in 1869. Daniel Quinlivan died in 1903, but Thomas carried on his own business advertising, "My system is founded on the teachings of anatomy and perfected in daily experience." (1995.41.6.)

The T.J. Southerland Horse Exchange was located at 109 North Second Street. The Orton Hotel carriage sits on the left. This photograph was taken c. 1890, when a private horse-car company "that provided fragmentary service" still operated. The lame firm was later purchased and transformed into the streetcar system. (1984.70.53.)

Handsome in its day, this turn-of-the-century building on the southeast corner of Fourth and Castle Streets was looking frayed in 1963 when this photograph was taken. Originally home to Melchoir George Tienken's "Palace Variety Store," it became William B. Beery Dry Goods in 1915; the local company eventually evolved into the present 20-store chain known as Belk-Beery. (1984.70.155.)

Henry Sternberger's misty photograph portrays Wilmington in 1945. The Motte Business College building is gone, as is the Snow's Esso Servicecenter's "Schlitz" sign. The Hill-Wright-Wootten House, in all its statuesque beauty, is next to St. James Church. (1985.72.7.)

By 19th-century standards, this Atlantic Coast Line office building was as generic as its name. Building A was one of several imposing railroad structures that dominated the west side of North Front Street, beyond Walnut, for 70 years. Though it was built in 1889, the tower was not added until 1900. (1983.79.7.)

Like Building A, Building B housed general offices of the Atlantic Coast Line. In 1960, corporate headquarters moved to Jacksonville, Florida, emptying downtown of 1,000 workers and transferring a $7 million payroll. In 1962, Building A and Building B were demolished. (1983.79.6.)

Union Station, built in 1913 on the northeast corner of Front and Red Cross Streets, was designed by Joseph F. Leitner, the official architect for the Atlantic Coast Line Railroad. It was a noisy place where the deafening harsh and shrill sounds of trains mixed with the periodic clanging of a large brass bell and the slow drone of metal baggage cart wheels rolling across the concrete floor. Neither that, nor the smell of the great engines, nor the coal soot that dusted it, was enough to rob the place of its magic. For years, it was Wilmington's best gateway to the wonders that lay in other places and the glamour of some of the passenger cars could make the trip a destination in itself. Several generations of Wilmingtonians felt the high drama of Union Station meeting loved ones, saying tearful goodbyes, welcoming VIPs, and leaving on the midnight train for a honeymoon trip to New York. Union Station was demolished July 11, 1970. (1980.42.129.)

Photographer Hugh Morton bravely snapped this picture of a 1953 fire at the Wilmington Terminal Warehouse as nitrate of soda, sugar, and tobacco burned with a vengeance. An anchor chain holds the ship, *Maxmanus*, which was moved away from the wharf when the fire began. Warehouse owner Peter Browne Ruffin was just thankful the wind was in the city's favor.

The J.W. Murchison Company, established in 1876 as Murchison and Giles, constructed this building in 1911–1912, on the southeast corner of Water and Chestnut Streets. Henry Bonitz was the architect, and Joseph Schad, the contractor for the three-story, 37,000-square-foot building. Suppliers of wholesale hardware, the firm served a retail market that spanned a 125-mile radius. Here, the building is being demolished, c. 1964. (1980.53.184.)

Union Bus Terminal, depicted here by local artist Sam Bissette, was located on the southwest corner of Second and Walnut Streets. It was built in 1938–39 by Eugene Blackwell Bugg, owner of the Hotel Wilmington. (Betty B. Crouch.)

No, St. James Church hasn't vanished, nor has the 1911 statue of George Davis. However, a generation of Wilmingtonians gleefully said Mr. Davis was pointing to a popular ABC store at 225 Market Street that was destroyed in 1961. This photograph was taken c. 1945. (1994.4.129.)

In 1939, Bruce Barclay Cameron Jr. put his new civil engineering degree from Virginia Military Institute to good use when he built this nationally acclaimed structure. Designed by E. Vance Florence and contracted by Robert Simon, the MacMillan and Cameron building was a gleaming sign that the Great Depression was history. (1982.18.67.)

In 1912, the Fidelity Development and Investment Company opened Sunset Park, a suburb southwest of Greenfield Lake. Architect Burrett Stephens designed some of the first homes in the neighborhood, but the styles changed as the burgeoning shipyard made housing more urgent. Here, the Philadelphia Nationals and Baltimore Orioles pose before an exhibition game on March 20, 1913. (1985.16.3.)

World War II brought soldiers and business to Holly Ridge when it grew to house 40,000 troops at Camp Davis. The Popkins family of nearby Jacksonville adopted the name "Boom Town" for their business, which is still in operation. Here, PFC Marshall Bobrow stands near the finance office where he worked, c. 1943. (1988.6.144.)

"Before the war, nobody in Holly Ridge was in a hurry because there wasn't anything to do. But that is ended now," reported the *Charlotte Observer* in 1941. There was plenty of work to do in places like Headquarters Building, pictured here, but for play, soldiers preferred Wilmington. Restaurants, bars, and pool halls prospered as local mothers lectured their eligible daughters about the sins of servicemen. (1988.6.61.)

The Plantation Club, located "three miles out" on the Carolina Beach Road, was a favorite nightspot during the war. Owners Abie Rubin and Henry Omirly made sure guests were treated to sophisticated fare and the best in band music. (1988.6.149.)

There's a good reason we call it "Monkey Junction." The owner of a service station on the west side of the Carolina Beach Road thought he would get more business if he kept a few monkeys around. Here, young Thurston Watkins makes a new acquaintance, c. 1939. A chain links the monkey to his tiny residence.

Four

ALONG THE SHORE

"Where we can live a life sublime in one unending summertime . . . ."
—William L. deRosset

The realm of the Cape Fear Museum covers many miles of shore and several famous beaches. Waterfront properties particularly are vulnerable to developers' bulldozers, hurricanes, northeasters, and, ironically, fire. These photographs are treasures, for the structures they portray proved to be no more permanent than the sand art seen here, sculpted by a medical student vacationing at Wrightsville Beach, c. 1940s, and photographed by Henry Sternberger. (1985.72.12.)

As seen in the bottom left panel, before the streetcar, the steam engine of the Wilmington and Sea Coast Train Company puffed across water and marsh from the mainland to the east side of the Hammocks, known today as Harbor Island. In this photograph, taken c. 1888, passengers are arriving near the location of the present drawbridge.

After paying Elijah Hewlett one dollar for the right-of-way, the Ocean View Railroad built new tracks and a trestle (seen in the top right photograph) to transport passengers from the Hammocks to Wrightsville Beach. The same company also built this "switchback," or roller coaster, that sat near the present site of the Oceanic Restaurant.

The Island Beach Hotel opened in 1888 at the Hammocks, a destination accessible only by boat and train. Victorian fashion must have put a damper on tanning, but at night, elegantly dressed couples crowded the ballroom dance floor. Proprietor Horace Platt didn't fool natives when he touted "hot and cold salt water baths" or when he announced that recent rains had "diminished the inconvenience" of a failed artesian well, but the hotel thrived anyway.

This photograph was taken about the time Mrs. Edward S. Latimer, who resided at 208 South Third Street, entertained 50 friends at a luncheon at the Island Beach Hotel. The event would have been typical of many held there.

"A special train was run, which left the Princess Street depot at 11:30 a.m. on January 23, 1889, and arrived at the Hammocks a half hour later. After strolling about the island, over the bridge, and down the beach, the party was called to luncheon in the dining hall at the Island Beach Hotel. The entire party returned to the city at 5:30 p.m., delighted with their jaunt," reported the *Messenger*. (1980.1.8.)

Cars and buses had rendered obsolete the Tidewater Power Company passenger station at Wrightsville Beach when this photograph was taken in 1950. Henry Bonitz designed the Spanish Mission-style depot in 1917; it was built by R.H. Brady for $5,000. The drawbridge on the left and Faircloth's Seafood Restaurant, which was famous for its listing floor, are also gone. (1992.117.3.)

This photograph was taken from the tower of the Oceanic Hotel, c. 1925. Hugh MacRae's company, Tidewater Power, owned the hotel, Lumina, the streetcar line, and the Harbor Island Pavilion. One advertisement covered a lot of business when guests at the Oceanic were offered "special cars on the electric road from the hotel door to Lumina" and a convention hall that was only "two minutes away." (1985.72.8.)

The Harbor Island Auditorium was built by the Tidewater Power Company in 1916. Large enough to seat 2,000 people, it was a popular convention site and movie theater. During World War I, the building was used for Navy training. Here, vacationing Shriners, harnessed temporarily by the camera, pose in 1920 for a group picture. (1987.23.19.)

A group of well-dressed beachgoers apply some adaptive use to the Tidewater Power Company's "interurban electricline" trestle at Banks Channel. The event seems to be part of the Feast of Lanterns, touted as "a week of unalloyed joy." In the 1920s, long before the current holiday flotilla, participants sailed their skiffs, which were decorated in Oriental motifs and flickering lamps, up and down Banks Channel.

The Seashore Hotel opened June 7, 1898, at Station Three on the beachcar line, the former site of the Old Brown Bathhouse. This photograph on the verandah was taken in 1910, the same year that the Seashore boasted a new steel pier. In the 1920s, the Seashore Hotel opened a miniature golf course on Banks Channel. (1990.66.10.)

In 1935, the Seashore Hotel was renamed the Ocean Terrace Hotel in a contest won by Virginia Bellamy, who received a $15 prize for her creativity. This photograph was taken by Hugh Morton c. 1945. Hurricane Hazel damaged the building in 1954; a year later, it burned to the ground. In 1964, it was replaced by the Blockade Runner. (1997.54.102.)

Someone had fun naming the Tarrymoore Hotel; it was probably the owner, W.J. Moore of Charlotte. Built in 1905, it was located at Station One, the beachcar's first stop at Wrightsville; it originally contained 125 rooms, a bowling alley, a ballroom, and card parlors. (1981.71.9.)

The Tarrymoore, sold in 1911, reopened in 1912 as the Oceanic Hotel, with 75 new rooms, a boardwalk, a pavilion, and an observatory tower, seen here, that "afforded the finest view of the Atlantic between Atlantic City and Florida." The hotel burned on January 28, 1934, in a fire that destroyed half the buildings at Wrightsville Beach, including the Solomon, Sternberger, and Bear cottages on the right. The children pictured are Samuel Nathan Bear and Janet Bear, c. 1922. (IA4797.)

Though the Tidewater Power and Light Company was the official owner of Lumina, many people contributed to its creation. The Nathan family of Wilmington, who owned the far south end of Wrightsville Beach, donated the tract on which the glowing pavilion was built. Hugh MacRae's daughter at Vassar, Agnes MacRae (Morton), named the structure. A teenager and a foreign language student, she had just learned the Latin word for light. Architect Henry E. Bonitz designed it to be a work of art and to function as both a casual recreation facility and an elegant dancing venue with a masterful natural sound system.

Lumina opened June 3, 1905, and was the most remote and entertaining destination on the streetcar line. During the day, outside activities were diverse, including beauty pageants, greased pole contests, canoe races, and swimming—an activity monitored by lifeguards always ready to leap into long six-seater surfboats for the rescue. At night, hundreds of exterior lights led the way to an almost magical ballroom that, for several decades, was the most elegant place to be on a Saturday night. In its heyday, the 120-foot-by-50-foot dance hall was usually filled to capacity with elegantly dressed young people sporting their best Victorian manners. Nationally known bands and a good public relations department brought people from as far as Atlanta and Richmond to the "pleasure palace" by the sea, to dance to the "syncopating music." Outside, silent movies were shown under the stars at the edge of the surf. "A more delightful setting could not be imagined," penned one overwrought writer. "With one's favorite star on the screen, and the strains of the orchestra mingling with the music of the waves, Romance is the Queen of the Hour."

Lumina had lost much of its brilliance by the 1920s, and by the time streetcar service was discontinued on April 27, 1940, it was simply an oceanside dance hall. When it was demolished in 1973, most of the original heart pine timber was still in excellent shape, despite its encounters with Hurricane Hazel and many other unnamed storms. One of the old Lumina timbers serves as a mantle in the home of Mr. and Mrs. Robert G. Greer, located at 1218 Country Club Road. (1984.70.68.)

SHELL ISLAND BEACH

The National Negro Playground

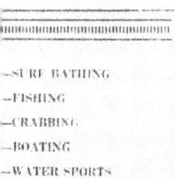

- SURF BATHING
- FISHING
- CRABBING
- BOATING
- WATER SPORTS

Shell Island BEACH

MORE THAN A RESORT

movement founded in the fore-
of liberal business men of the
to realize that the negro's out-
social and recreational develop-
s heretofore been severely lim-

ISLAND REMOVES THAT LIMIT!

Prospective beach dwellers who desire lots, cottages, rooms, business sites, concessions or information, should apply to

HOME REALTY CO.
Fiscal Agents

124 Princess Street   Wilmington, N. C.

Fast, Regular Car Schedule Direct Without Delay...

Shell Island BEACH

—Increases the list of things in w
North Carolina negroes lead. It is
only exclusive colored resort of its
in the world! In the first (1923)
son visitors have come from 50 citi
10 states, ranging from New York
Alabama.

SEVERAL CONVENTIONS FOR THE SEAS

Wilmington developers C.B. Parmele and Thomas H. Wright developed a resort for African Americans on Shell Island in 1923. R.R. Stone of Stone Towing supplied the ferryboat and a pier near Moore's Inlet, and Luther T. Rogers built the pavilion seen above. Dr. Frank W. Avant, an African-American physician, was the chief organizer of events on the island, including performances by jazz musicians Lindsey Brown and John Cabbage Walter.

During its first summer in operation, Shell Island Resort attracted visitors from ten states, but the majority of the tourists were Wilmingtonians who caught the streetcar at Tenth and Campbell Streets and rode it to a station on the northern shore of Harbor Island. In 1926, fire destroyed the entire development. These Shell Island cottages were photographed in 1924. (*Wilmington Star News.*) (IA1725.)

Edgar Yow, a white Wilmington attorney, conceived the idea of a beach developed by African Americans for African Americans. African-American businessman Wade Chestnut executed the plan, developing property north of Surf City as Ocean City Beach. Established in 1949, Ocean City contained about 100 houses by 1979.

Monte Carlo by the Sea was owned by Frank and Lula Freeman Hill, residents of an African-American resort known as Seabreeze. Located just north of Carolina Beach, Seabreeze attracted thousands of tourists on summer holidays during the 1920s and 1930s. This photograph was taken c. 1950. (IA3077.)

Sedgeley Hall, a Carolina Beach club named for an old plantation, was built in 1898, not long before this photograph was taken. Captain John W. Harper, who owned a railroad and a steamer to Carolina Beach, donated the land; Henry Bonitz designed the building. Early members included James Reilly, Thomas H. Wright, Fred Kidder, James Cowan, and William French. (1987.23.23.)

The roof garden of the 1916 Greystone Inn (right foreground) at Carolina Beach had a retractable roof to shield dancers and orchestras from the rain. The new Bame Hotel (right, rear) reopened in 1941 after a 1940 fire burned an older hotel and ignited scores of beach buildings, including a firing range that was stocked with 8,000 rounds of ammunition. (1993.10.7.)

A year after Sedgeley Hall burned in 1910, a new 13,000-square-foot pavilion emerged. Henry Bonitz again served as architect and W.B. Bevill as contractor. The 14-foot-wide porch allowed Captain Harper's beach train, the *Shoo Fly*, to deposit passengers onto the premises. (1993.10.7.)

In 1943, local artist Claude Howell (standing on porch), Charles Freeburn, Marshall, Margaret Fraser (on steps), and journalist and promoter Bill Keziah camped out for three days in this ill-fated fisherman's shack on Bald Head Island. Two years later, Mr. Keziah attempted to make the island headquarters for the newly formed United Nations Organization. (1997.55.471.)

Bibliography

Angley, Wilson. *A History of Fort Johnston of the Lower Cape Fear*. Southport, NC: 1996.
Bishir, Catherine W. *North Carolina Architecture*. (Photographs by Tim Buchman.) Chapel Hill: 1990.
Block Books and Deed Transfer Records, New Hanover County Courthouse.
Campbell, Walter E. *Across Fortune's Tracks: A Biography of William Rand Kenan, Jr*. Chapel Hill: 1996.
Boney, Leslie N. Jr., ed. with historical sketches by James L. Allegood. *Cape Fear Club (1967–1983)*. Wilmington: 1984.
Cashman, Diane Cobb. *Cape Fear Adventure*. Woodland Hills, CA: 1982.
———. *The Cape Fear Country Club, 1896–1996*. Wilmington: 1996.
———. *Headstrong, The Biography of Amy Morris Bradley (1823–1904)*. Wilmington: 1990.
Evans, W. McKee. *Ballots and Fence Rails*. Durham: 1966.
Fales, Robert. *Memories Yesteryear*. Wilmington: 1988.
Fonvielle, Chris E. Jr. *Fort Anderson: Battle for Wilmington*. Mason City, IA: 1999.
———. *The Wilmington Campaign: Last Days of Departing Hope*. Campbell, CA: 1997.
Funk, Ruth Christy. 175th Anniversary Project. Transcribed tapes memories of First Presbyterian Church.
Gunter, S. Carol. *Carolina Heights Preservation of an Urban Neighborhood in Wilmington, North Carolina*. Wilmington: 1982.
Hall, Lewis Philip. *Land of the Golden River, I*. Wilmington: 1975.
———. *Land of the Golden River, II, III*. Wilmington, 1980.
Herring, Ethel and Carolee Williams. *Fort Caswell: In War and Peace*. Wendell, NC: 1983.
Hewlett, Crockette W. and Mona Smalley. *Between the Creeks, Revised Masonboro Sound, 1735–1985*. Wilmington: 1985.
How North Carolina Grew. W.P.A. Raleigh: 1850.
Howe, Samuel. *American Country Houses of Today*. New York: 1915.
Howell, Andrew J. *The Book of Wilmington*.
Jones, Walter Burgwin. *The Jones-Burgwin Family History*. Montgomery: 1913.
Kernan, Charles. *Rails to Weeds*. 1989.
Lathrop, Elise. *Early American Inns and Taverns*. New York: 1926.
Lee, Lawrence. *A History of Brunswick County, North Carolina*. Charlotte: 1980.
———. *The Lower Cape Fear in Colonial Days*. Chapel Hill: 1965.
Lower Cape Fear Historical Society Archives. Family files. Subject files.
MacMillan, Emma Woodward. *Wilmington's Vanished Homes and Buildings*. Raleigh: 1966.
McKoy, Elizabeth F. *Early New Hanover County Records*. Wilmington: 1973.
McKoy, Henry B. *Wilmington, North Carolina—Do You Remember When?*. Greenville, SC: 1957.
The Memoirs of Joseph Gardner Swift. Worcester, MA: 1890.
Pictorial Sketch of Wilmington, North Carolina and Vicinity. New Hanover County Library.
Rankin, D. Helen and E. Charles Nelson, eds. *Curious in Everything: The Career of Arthur Dobbs of Carrickfergus (1689–1765.)* Carrickfergus, Northern Ireland: 1990.
Reaves, William M. *Strength Through Struggle: The Chronological and Historical Record of the African-American Community in Wilmington, North Carolina, 1865–1950*. Wilmington: 1998.
Riley, Jack. *Carolina Power and Light, 1908–1958*. Raleigh: 1958.
Russell, Anne. *Wilmington: A Pictorial History*. Norfolk, VA: 1981.
Scott, Sir Walter. *The Antiquary*. http//eng.hss.cum.edu/fiction/the-antiquary.txt
Seapker, Janet K. and Edward F. Turberg. "Historic Architecture of the Cape Fear." Text for lecture series, 1995.
Shaffer, E.T.H. *Carolina Gardens*. New York: 1963.
———."Smith's Creek Bridge fell in yesterday." (Entire report) *Wilmington Post*. October 8, 1873.
Sprunt, James. *Chronicles of the Lower Cape Fear*. Wilmington: 1992.
Wilmington Morning Star.
Stick, David. *Bald Head*. Wendell, NC: 1985.

Turberg, Edward F. *A History of American Building Technology*. Durham: 1981.
Watkins, Greg. *Wrightsville Beach: A Pictorial History*. Wrightsville Beach: 1997.
Watson, Alan D., Dennis R. Lawson, and Donald R. Lennon. *Harnett, Hooper and Howe*. Wilmington: 1979.
Wrenn, Tony P. *Wilmington, North Carolina: An Architectural and Historical Portrait*. Charlottesville, VA: 1984. Subject and Family Files-Lower Cape Fear Historical Society Archives.
The State, 15 May 1969. (MacRae Castle.)

Photograph Donors

Photograph donors include the following: the Lower Cape Fear Historical Society, the New Hanover County Public Library, the University of North Carolina, Duke University, the North Carolina Division of Archives and History, the U.S. Postal Service, the City of Wilmington, the Columbus County Historical Society, Melva Calder, Jean Graham, Howard Loughlin, Louise deRosset Smith, Caroline Newbold Swails, the *Wilmington Star News*, Barbara Marcroft, Anne McKoy Parks, Katherine McKoy Ehling, John B. Green, Hugh Morton, Henry Bacon McKoy, Barbara Rowe, Johanna Duls Wooten, Ida Brooks Kellam, Richard Wells, Frances Loughlin, Larry B. Lee, Dr. James R. Lee, Barbara Bear Jamison, Fred and Susan Block, Tabitha Hutaff McEachern, Claude Howell, Joanne Corbett, Sandra Corbett Hiatt, Ethel V. Botesky, Frances Hearn Grover, Lucile S. Goldberg, Laura H. Norden Schorr, Andrew J. Howell, Betty Bugg Crouch, Emma Woodward MacMillan, Mary McCarl Wilson, Catherine Solomon, Marie S. Kahn, Betty Foy Taylor, David E. Franks, Martin and Gibbs Willard, First Citizen's Bank (William Golder), David Wilson, Richard H. Wells, Augusta M. Cooper, Thurston Watkins, C.H. and H.O. MacDonald, E.A. Swain, Regina King, Ann Russell, Glendora and Wilbur Gore, Alice Lee Bulluck, Sarah Godwin, Gerald N. Dunn, Dave Milns, Leora H. McEachern, Naomi Sullivan, Arthur Bluethenthal, Frank Hill, Steve McAllister, Bebe S. Thompson, Eloise R. Cherry, Margaret Stallworth, Douglas Fox, Robert Hall, Caronell C. Chestnut, Peggy Moore Perdew, and A. Jarvis Wood.

Photographers whose work is featured in this publication include Hugh Morton, Louis T. Moore, Melva Calder, Freda Wilkins, Eric Norden, James Swails, Charles A. Farrell, Barbara Marcroft, Margaret Groover, Charles E. Vale, C. Yates and A. Orr, Rufus Morgan, George Nevens, Burnett and Lewis, John Kelly, Sarah Godwin, William B. McKoy, Henry Bacon McKoy, Henry Sternberger, and Ethel V. Botesky.

Index

Abrams, Aaron, 93
Ahrens, Benjamin H.J., 28
Airlie, 40, 44, 46, 47, 48
American Missionary Association, 66
Anderson, Edwin, 42, 43
Atlantic Coast Line, 79, 106, 107
Bacon, Henry, 7, 31, 32
Bald Head Island, 52, 124
Bame Hotel, 123
Bank of Cape Fear, 88
Bank of New Hanover, 60, 89
Bear, Isaac, 68
Bear, Samuel, 36, 68, 71, 101
Belk-Beery, 22, 105
Bellamy, John D., 27, 90
Bellamy, Robert R., 25, 102
Bellamy, Virginia, 118
Bellamy, Dr. W.J.H., 70

Bijou Theater, 21, 44, 96, 97, 98
Blockade Runner Hotel, 118
Block's Cantfade Shirts, 99
Boney, Leslie N., 78
Bonitz, Henry, 31, 32, 36, 84, 87, 103, 108, 115, 120, 123, 124
Bowden family, 9, 35
Bradley, Amy, 24
Brady, R.H., 74, 97, 115
Bridgers, Mary, 57
Brunswick Hotel, 73
Brunswick Town, 10
Bugg, Eugene Blackwell, 93, 109
Burgwin, Captain J.H.K., 12, 13, 88
Burgwin, John, 12, 88
Burnett, Dr. Foster, 72
C.D. Maffitt's Supply House, 84, 85
Camp Davis, 99, 111

Cape Fear Country Club, 78
Carolina Beach, 122-124
Champion Compress, 85, 86, 100
Chestnut, Wade, 121
City Market, 34
Community Hospital, 72
Cooper, Augusta Moseley, 100
Cornelius Harnett School, 64
Corbett, W.A., 48
David, Abram, 28
Dawson, James, 19, 88
Dawson, John, 14, 88, 91
Delgado Mills, 102
deRosset, Captain A.L.,
deRosset, Armand, 12, 15, 59, 77, 95
Dickinson, Platt K., 23, 77
Dobbs, Arthur, 10, 11, 12
East Wilmington School, 64
Eshcol, 42, 43
Evans, Minnie and Julius, 47
Farrell, Charles A., 45
Federal Point Lighthouse, 52
Fifth Avenue Methodist Church, 58
Finian, 43
First Church of Christ Scientist, 57
First Presbyterian Church, 39, 60, 61, 62, 70
Flagler, Henry, 103
Flagler, Mary Lily Kenan, 74, 75
Fonvielle, Dr. Chris, 51
Formyduval School, 63
Fort Caswell, 51
Fort Fisher, 18, 52
Freret, W.A., 54
Front Street Methodist Church, 57, 58, 87
Frying Pan Lightship, 53
Gardner, Benjamin, 80
Gause, James F., 78
Gause, Drs. Suzette and Roger, 72
Gieschen Brothers Atlantic Inn, 99
Goldberg, Lucile Sternberger, 37
Grace Methodist Church, 58
Grainger, Isaac Bates, 19, 88
Greenfield Lake, 20, 93, 97, 110
Greenville Sound, 41
Gregory Community School, 67
Greystone Inn, 123
Hall, Dr. B. Frank, 61, 95
Hanson, Louis A., 82
Harbor Island, 114–117, 121
Harnett, Cornelius, 11
Harper, Capt. John, 123, 124
Harper Sanitorium, 71

Harriss, George, 26, 60
Hemenway School, 65
Hermitage, 12, 13
Hewlett, Addison, 103
Hewlett, Elijah, 114
Heyer Building, 90
Heyer, Matt, 35
Hicks, Rufus William, 20
Hill-Wright-Wootten House, 16, 17, 105
Hilton, 11
Holt-Wise House, 40, 102
Hotel Wilmington, 93, 109
Howard, J.H. "Foxy", 96, 97, 98
Howe, Alfred, 81
Howe, Valentine, Sr., 71
Howell, Claude, 39, 61, 124
Hutaff, George, 28
Isaac Bear School, 68
Island Beach Hotel, 116
J.H. Rehder and Company, 33
James Walker Memorial Hospital, 25, 70, 71
Jones, Pembroke, 23, 33, 34, 40, 44, 45, 46, 47
Kenan, William Rand, 74
Kidder, Edward, 2, 20, 77, 103
Lazarus, Aaron, 19
Lee, Lawrence, 10
Lumina, 8, 115, 120
Lynch, James B., 69, 72, 103, 110
MacMillan and Cameron, 38, 110
MacMillan, Henry, 61
MacRae, Alexander, 29, 30, 31
MacRae Castle, 30-32
MacRae, Hugh, 29, 31, 115, 120
Maffitt, Clarence Dudley, 84
Marcroft, Barbara, 33, 47
Market House, 80, 81
Maynard, 11
McCarl, Helen Weathers, 61
McEachern, Tabitha Hutaff, 28
McKoy House, 81
McKoy, Elizabeth F., 7
McKoy, Henry Bacon, 50, 61, 85
McKoy, James F., 7
McKoy, William Berry, 7, 21
McKoy, Mrs. William H., 41
McMichael, J.M. 62
McMillan, Dugald, 77
McMillen, Charles, 28, 36, 74
Meares, John L., 77
Metts, Capt. James, 75
Miller, James Alfred Locke, Jr., 17
Monk Barns, 41

Monkey Junction, 112
Monte Carlo by the Sea, 122
Moody, Dwight L., 86
Moore, Louis T., 35
Moore, Maurice, 12
Moore, Nathaniel, 17
Moore, Roger, 35
Moore, W.J., 119
Morton, Hugh, 53, 108, 118
Moseley, Levi McKoy, 100
Mount Lebanon, 16, 46
Mount Lebanon Chapel, 16
Mrs. Potter's Boarding House, 14
Murchison, J.W., 54, 108
Murphy, Dr. J.G., 39
Nakina, 63
Niestlies Drug Store, 72
Norris, John, 50, 80, 88
Oakdale Cemetery, 32, 76, 77, 88
Ocean City Beach, 122
Ocean Terrace Hotel, 118
Ocean View Railroad, 114
Oceanic Hotel, 115, 119
Odd Fellows Building, 103
Omirly, Henry, 112
Orton Hotel, 89, 92, 93, 104
Orton Plantation, 17, 92
Parmele, C.B., 121
Parsley, Agnes MacRae, 31, 32
Parsley, Walter L., 32
Pearsall, Oscar, 95
Plantation Club, 112
Pope, John Russell, 44, 45, 46
Post, James F., 26, 30, 54, 57, 65, 77, 81
Price's Creek Lighthouse, 52
Queen of Mondigo, 29
Quinlivan, Daniel and Thomas, 104
Reaves, William M., 49
Rehder, Carl, 97
Rehder, Henry, 34
Rehder, John H., 33, 34, 91
Royal Theater, 98
Ruffin, Peter Browne, 108
Russellborough, 10
Ruth Hall, 78
St. James Church, 56, 59, 88, 105, 109
St. John's Episcopal Church, 59
Sam Jones Tabernacle, 56
Seabreeze, 122
Seashore Hotel, 118
Sedgeley Hall, 123, 124
Shell Island Resort, 121

Sloan, Samuel, 60, 89
Sol. Bear and Company, 99
Solomon House, 32
Southern Building, 35, 90
Southport, 52, 74, 94
Southside Baptist Church, 62
Alexander Sprunt and Son, 83, 86, 87, 100
Sprunt, James, 15, 29, 70, 71, 74, 82, 86, 94, 103
Sprunt, William H., 25, 71
Stephens, Burrett, 40, 65, 90, 97, 98, 110
Sternberger, Henry, 98, 105, 113
Stuart, Kate, 94
Sue McGinney Gregg House, 63
Sunset Park, 110
Swann-Weathers House, 38
T.J. Southerland Horse Exchange, 104
Tarrymoore Hotel, 119
Taylor, Col. Walker, 74, 75
Temple of Israel, 36
Tidewater Power and Light Co., 105, 115, 117, 120
U.S. Custom House, 50, 54
U.S. Marine Hospital, 69, 70
U.S. Post Office, 50, 53, 54, 55, 63, 98
Union Bus Terminal, 109
Union Station, 99, 107
University of North Carolina at Wilmington, 48, 68
Vollers, Luhr H., 34, 37
Walker, James, 60, 70, 92
Wallace, Mary Borden, 24
Watkins, Thurston, 112
Weathers, C.M., 28
Weil, Ella, 40
Wells, Percy, 96, 97, 98
Willard, Martin S., 61, 90
William H. Green and Co., 91
Williston Industrial Schools, 66, 67
Wilmington and Weldon Railroad, 17, 23, 57
Wilmington Iron Works, 39
Wilmington Terminal Warehouse, 108
Wood, Edward Jenner, 22
Wood, J.A., 92
Wood, John Coffin, 30, 57
Wood, Robert B., 57
Wood, Thomas Fanning, 22
Worth and Worth, 83
Wright, Thomas H. (1876–1956), 41, 68, 121, 123
Wright, William Augustus, 17, 26, 77, 102
Wrightsville Beach, 8, 45, 113–120
Young Men's Christian Association, 73

www.ingramcontent.com/pod-product-compliance
Lightning Source LLC
Chambersburg PA
CBHW080852100426
42812CB00007B/2000